THE UNSTOPPABLE
ENTREPRENEUR
THE EMPOWERING TRUTH ABOUT SUCCESS

STEPHEN & RACHEL JACKSON

Foreword by Dana Derricks & Akbar Sheikh

Copyright

Foreword

FROM THE DESK OF DANA DERRICKS

CLEAR LAKE, WISCONSIN

It was 10:07pm on a Tuesday night. I was a 20-year-old college kid, having just finished a 4-hour night class. I was in line at Taco Bell...starving. I got to the counter and placed my order, excited to be able to wrap up a long day with a meal before heading home to pass out.

"That'll be six dollars and twelve cents", said the young clerk.

I handed him my card and watched him swipe it, then he swiped it a second time, and then a third.

After the third time, he looked at me, puzzled, and said, "It's saying 'card declined'".

Horrified, I reached in my pocket to see if I had any cash. I didn't. I reached over and grabbed my card, then lied and said out loud, "Dang, I think something's not working right...I'll have to call my bank". My chest was tight. My voice cracked. I was red and sweaty. As I walked out, empty-handed and with an empty stomach, I had a realization. I knew what had happened. I was broke. Dead broke. I didn't even have $6 to feed myself. You can feel the embarrassment and shame I felt, can't you? From that day on, I made a promise to NEVER allow myself to get in a position even CLOSE to that moment, ever again.

Fast-forward just shy of a decade...and I've made good on that promise. I've been fortunate enough to accomplish more than most dream of. I'm an entrepreneur that's been featured on Forbes, Entrepreneur Magazine, Inc., and many others. I've won high-honor entrepreneurial awards, including making over $4 million in sales online. Most importantly, though, I've been able to coach, train, and inspire tens of thousands of entrepreneurs from more than 61 countries to pursue their purpose, as well.

I'm not supposed to have done that. I'm just a farm kid from a tiny town in Wisconsin. Truthfully, none of that was possible without that evening at Taco Bell, when I was completely defeated. If I can do this, so can you. I won't lie, there were more situations than I care to remember that I didn't know if I'd ever get through. The reality is this: being an entrepreneur isn't pretty. It isn't all expensive cars, gorgeous women, and all the glamour those gurus out there want to lead us to believe. Not even close.

It's actually about weathering storms, facing problems head on, and running TOWARD the fire… not away from it. In fact, I'll go as far as saying that not everybody is cut out to be an entrepreneur. If you can't handle criticism, adversity, and getting the rug pulled from under you…time and time again…you won't make it as an entrepreneur.

The good news?

You're closer than ever to the resources and people that you need in your corner. For almost a decade, I struggled. I felt alone. I almost gave up, more than once. I wish I would have met Stephen and Rachel a decade ago. What's easy to remember is that for every ten folks that tell you that you can't, or you won't there is still that one who says you CAN and you WILL. Let that person be the catalyst for you.

The truth is that you are NOT alone.… and there's absolutely nothing wrong with you. You're you for a reason, and you've got talent inside of you that the world needs to be blessed with. They need to see your face. They need to hear your message. They need YOU.

This book WILL change your life and give you both the courage and permission to achieve your wildest dreams, if you let it. In an online world filled with more phonies than real folks, you've found a gem in this book. Let it be your internal compass toward a life not of flash and glamour, but of fulfillment and purpose. We're here for you, keep going.

You CAN. You WILL.

You can find more about Dana and his amazing resources for entrepreneurs at: *www.DanaDerricks.com*

From the Desk of Akbar Sheikh

Irving, Texas

I am privileged and honored Stephen and Rachel, have asked me to write one of the forewords for their book.

The topic is simple. Unstoppable entrepreneurs are fulfilled entrepreneurs. What's fascinating about that is they go hand in hand because a fulfilled entrepreneur actually equals an unstoppable entrepreneur.

I just wrapped up a sold-out event in Sydney and there was a lot of Imposter Syndrome in the room. Imposter Syndrome is when you think that you're not worthy of teaching or selling anything to anyone. Here's the reality.

If God has gifted you with the tools and the skills to actually help people and really solve their problem, isn't it your molecular responsibility to do it? Shouldn't you do everything in your power to reach out to everyone who needs your solution? If you did, then what would we get—solved problems, entrepreneurs moving on, growing, making more so they can give more? This is the ripple effect that impacts families, communities and charities hence making the world a better place.

You see, once you get in that mindset, you are no longer selling—you're serving. Then you're coming from a place of servitude. You've decided to humbly accept the gifts that God has given you and use them for good.

If you're selling, then you're in the wrong business. You're doing the wrong thing. You need to be serving, and if you have a purpose that makes this world a better place you are a fulfilled entrepreneur. Now you're unstoppable.

I want you to read this book but remember that

it isn't some romantic novel for your entertainment. This is a blueprint, a guide to becoming unstoppable but nothing will happen unless you implement what you find in these pages.

Don't just read, I want you to implement. I want you to read a few pages, put it down and implement. Then read a few more pages, put it down, and implement.

Don't speed read through in an hour and say, "I'm all finished, that was a great book."

No, invest the time, do the work, implement the changes and you won't be disappointed.

I'm telling you these guys are really smart. Rachel and Stephen are very smart. They feed the world with their light, they want you to do the same, and so do I.

I'll see you on the top.

You can find more about Akbar and his amazing resources for entrepreneurs over at:

www.akbarsheikh.com

Table of Contents

Intro -- 15

Unstoppable --- 19

Step 1 Determining a Baseline ------------------------------------ 25

    THE LIFE CIRCLE -- 27

Step 2 Identifying Root Motivations ----------------------------37

    7 LEVELS -- 39
    THE PERFECT DAY --- 55

Step 3 Honing Your Strengths ----------------------------------- 65

    HIDDEN SUPER POWERS-------------------------------------- 67
    BUILDING A TEAM --- 85
    GIVING --- 95

Step 4 The Funnel Four --- 99

    ENVIRONMENT ---101

Conclusion---121

Acknowledgements---125

Dedication

For Whitney Golie, Michael Moore, and Katie Rogers.

Your struggle was not in vain.

"Deep in their roots, all flowers keep the light."
– Theodore Roethke

Intro

How would it feel to reach your full potential? To win big—despite past mistakes and setbacks? What would it feel like to conquer your giants and bring to life the dreams of your heart?

What if you knew you would live fulfilled and confident the rest of your life despite the uncertainty of tomorrow? To know the future you'd always hoped for wasn't just possible—but inevitable?

We all want to be the hero of our own story—to rise above mediocrity to the pinnacle of success. We long to find the inner strength to finally breakthrough, especially in our businesses. We want to be *The Unstoppable Entrepreneur's*, but most days we hardly feel like it.

What is the secret of unbreakable determination? Unrelenting will? Where do these businessmen and women get their unending perseverance? Those that built their brand from the ground up, these juggernauts of vision, were not born blessed to get ahead. They learned, and grew and became a force to reckon with, just like you will.

The truth is you're not as far off as you might think. In fact, you're only four-steps away from your unstoppable future. My wife and I have built a business on our passion; building *The Unstoppable Entrepreneur*.

Throughout our journey we encountered thousands of motivated, dedicated, all-in leaders many of whom are 6, 7, and 8 figure earners. Out of this tribe of incredible entrepreneurs there are those who gave everything; their health, their relationships, their finances to an idea of success that wasn't a true reflection of their values. Many of them lost in business, but all of them lost in life.

Others have found a better way—the road less traveled. Leaders who have become unstoppable and redefined success for themselves and have triumphantly built a business that genuinely supports that definition.

What if that's what true success is? And what starts us on the path to becoming unstoppable? Constructing a life built on what you love as defined by the individual.

Sure, you can have a generalized picture of success wrapped up in a couple hundred-thousand Instagram followers who gawk over the outrageous and luxurious. But when the dust settles and no one's around, you're left with your own life. It's just you and your definition of success and fulfillment.

Success is defined by you and only you. Whether it's having a corner office on the top floor of a skyscraper, making more so you can give your money to orphans in Thailand, or serving on your children's P.T.A. it all comes down to your individual stamp of SUCCESS.

There is no One-Size-Fits-All-Blueprint to success and fulfillment. Instead it's individuals willing to work through this four-step process for themselves, because every blueprint must be personally realized.

Let this book be your breath of fresh air, defibrillator shock, and paradigm shift to an unstoppable future.

Vulnerability will become your faithful ally. All your doubts and let downs will be your launching pad.

Have courage and peel back the lies. Take down the safety nets. Wipe off the makeup.

We've made it our mission to build *Unstoppable Entrepreneur's*. Today, if you choose to face yourself, your past, your abilities without judgment, then you can become unstoppable in any venture, but it comes at a cost. A cost we encourage you to pay now. Face the inner corridors of your mind and fight back the temptation to compromise or settle on a mediocre half-lived life.

Your dreams and passions are worthy of your time and energy.

Do you want to win in life? Then let us lead you on the better way— the road less traveled. It's calling your name.

You're only four-steps away.

Unstoppable

UN · STOP · PA · BLE

IMPOSSIBLE TO STOP OR PREVENT, CONTINUOUS.

I, (Stephen), was on the tail end of a failing, family business. I'll spare you the details and suffice it to say that the outcome was out of my control, even though I gave blood, sweat, time and tears.

During the decline of this venture, month after month we had eviction notices on our apartment door. When the business completely fell apart, we were hung out to dry being owed over ten thousand dollars in back wages. My jeep was repossessed. Credit destroyed. It was devastating.

Broke, broke, broke--but NOT broken!!! Became our motto. In many ways the crisis brought my wife and I closer, because even when we had nothing, we still had each other.

I wish you could have seen her face when I said that if I was going to be poor and miserable, I was going to do it on my own terms. In other words, "Hey, babe! Let's start a business!"

She was less than thrilled, but still completely supported my dream anyway.

We couldn't get much lower than rock bottom. I felt tremendous pressure to solve our financial problems as fast as possible. The way I saw it. I had two choices. First, I could have bought into the idea of success that had been thrust on me by my culture and society. At that point in my life the expectation was for me to take a sales job in upper-middle management and faithfully plug away from nine to five for the next twenty years. There's nothing wrong with this option except that I had already done it and felt like it was a step back into something that wouldn't challenge me and wouldn't go far to fix what was broken in our finances.

The second choice was to go with my gut, risk big and take my fate into my own hands. I knew I could break through the barriers and setbacks that had destroyed our finances.

I was standing at crossroads in my life. I could go get a J-O-B and dig my way out of the financial ruin a paycheck at a time, or I could shoot for the sky and start my own business. I knew that I could succeed as an entrepreneur, but I felt very much alone. My decision to start up a financial consulting and retirement planning business was seen as irresponsible by many of the people I loved and respected. It was not the right thing that I should have done. At least until it worked, and my income quadrupled in the first year. Suddenly, I was the rock star that people always knew would succeed.

My pride would love for that to be the whole story, but financial success wasn't the magic fix I'd hoped it would be. Don't get me wrong, money fixes a lot of things, and makes a lot of other things possible but after the first few years making the big bucks wasn't enough to get me motivated. I needed more, and I didn't know how to find it. I just knew I wasn't happy with the way my life and business had gone.

I was traveling and working way too much. I missed birthdays and anniversaries every year. My wife and I were growing further and further apart because I was hardly around and when I was around, I wasn't available. All the effort and sacrifice I put into my business was leaving me less and less fulfilled and to make matters even more interesting I kept a fourteen-year addiction to alcohol, gambling and drug use swept under the rug. The truth was that I needed real solutions for the issues I faced as a business owner, and human being.

I was living someone else's success story and it was making me sick. I knew there was more out there for me but no matter how hard I hustled I couldn't break through. Every success began to feel like one more nail in my coffin. It all came to a head in a hotel room one morning down in beautiful Santa Fe, New Mexico.

Again, I was faced with two choices. Stay the same and accept that achievement without fulfillment was the best I could have. This meant a hurting family life where I woke up discouraged and depressed every morning and toughed out my future. Just thinking about it felt so hopeless but it would save me from facing the other option, real soul deep change.

I could seek change and start a journey that at the time felt even more terrifying than beginning my first business from rock bottom. That was the day I stopped in my tracks and decided to find fulfillment--no matter what the cost.

I stopped chasing the American dream and started digging for real solutions. I had to slow down and take a look at the man in the mirror. Yeah, I had to look at me… I began to journey towards my own thoughts and desires. A journey that eventually resulted in the writing of this book.

The Unstoppable Entrepreneur is your guidebook for the success you've always desired. I wrote it because I believe in you. I want you to go with your gut, and breakthrough your barriers and setbacks. But I want you to be happy when you get there. I want you to know deep inside that you're on the right track and absolutely fulfilled in your business and life, every step of the way.

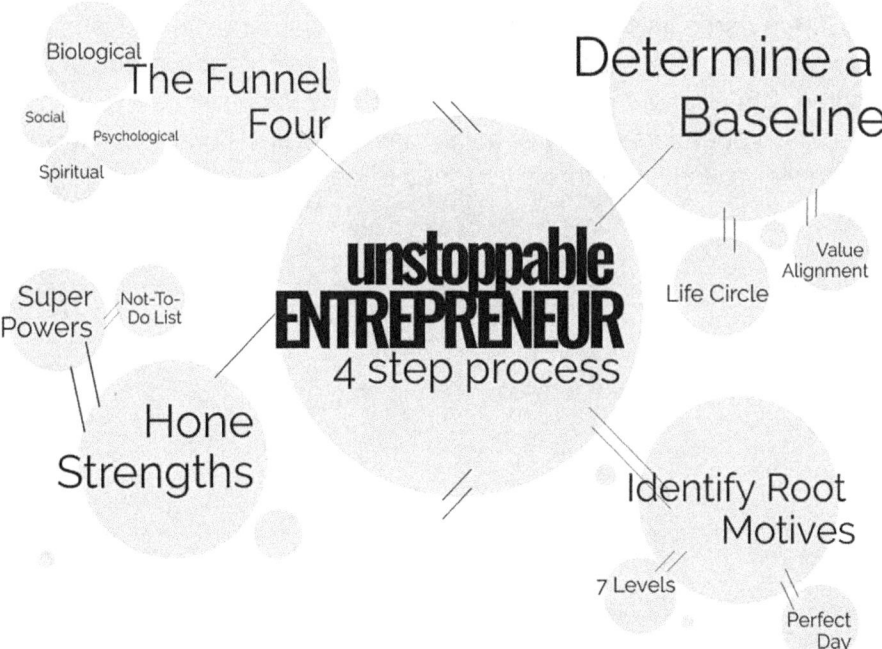

If you're willing, the four-step process will become your advocate.

First, we will determine your baseline. This is where we will break through misconceptions and false belief patterns heaped on us over the years. After this step you will know exactly where you are in relation to where you want to be. And without any hesitation you will know exactly what you want.Then we move right into identifying exactly what motivates you. For most of us these motivations are not on the surface or easily recognizable in our lives, making them ambiguous and hard to access. We'll show you the secret to unearth what moves you and unleash it to bring your dreams and goals to fruition.

In the third step, honing your strengths, we'll show you how to put your innate talents and gifts to work, and prove why you need to stop working on your weaknesses. We'll help you identify and optimize your superpowers and show you how to properly vet and hire the support that is going to take you to the next level.

Finally, we're going to bring it all together in The Funnel Four, where we optimize your environments to make your dreams inevitable.

By the end of this process you will have a clearer picture of who you are, what you want, and how you'll get it. This four-step process has worked with all of our clients, from Wall Street Executives to excavation equipment operators to stay-at-home moms and small business owners. These steps work, and this is your day to begin!

Biological

The Funnel

Social

Four

Psychological

Spiritual

Super   Not-To-
Powers   Do List

UN
ENTRE

4 st

Hone
Strengths

Step 1
Determining a Baseline

THE LIFE CIRCLE

Nobody likes pain, lack, or failure. I know I don't. It's human nature to stay as far away from suffering as possible. It's why most of us know more about what we want to avoid than where we want to arrive, and that mindset isn't doing any of us any favors. Living your life to avoid what you don't want won't get you where you want to go.

Let's say you and I meet up tomorrow in New York city at Times Square. Parked on the curb is a mint condition 2009 cherry red Ferrari F430. Next to it is a "non-descript" old beater. I will be leaving to an undisclosed location and I want you to find me. In two weeks I want you to meet me anywhere but the state of New York. At 12 o'clock I'm going to let you choose between one of two envelopes; both contain car keys and instructions. In the first envelope are keys to the Ferrari with instructions to drive it away from New York City for two weeks. If by chance you are able to meet up with me at an undisclosed location you will win the car and a million dollars. You cannot contact or track me and there are no hints or riddles to give you my location. Just blind chance and dumb luck.

I'm no statistician but I'm pretty sure your chances of winning the million and keeping the Ferrari are slim to none if you choose envelope one. And it's not the car's fault. The F430 has a top speed in excess of 196 mph and can accelerate from 0 to 60 mph in 3.6 seconds. That car could take you just about anywhere—fast and in style.

In the second envelope are keys to the beater and detailed instructions guiding you to the San Francisco Bridge with an itinerary of hotels, restaurants and gas stations to use along the way.

If you are able to meet me there before the two weeks are up, I'll trade the old beater for the Ferrari and give you a million dollars.

Both vehicles will move you away from New York City. Even with the less impressive vehicle, it's safe to say we'd meet up at the San Francisco Bridge with time to spare. You'd be a million dollars richer and driving a new Ferrari back home.

That's why knowing where you are and where you want to be are more important than knowing what you want to avoid.

We can tend to become fixated on our vehicle of success, whether it's our business model, products, delivery, etc... when what actually matters is our destination. Any running vehicle can get you where you want to go. Where do you want it to take you?

It still baffles me how many of us trudge through our lives with little to no thought of our end game. We're so focused on avoiding failure

and choosing the right vehicle for our success and at the same time we give little to no thought to our ultimate destination. We all want the flashy sports car of overnight success but without parameters we're just as ambiguous as a cherry red Ferrari blasting through the countryside hoping to win by chance and luck alone. We don't know where we are going or if we're going to even like where we end up, but man, we're going to get there fast!

- Where are you going?
- What do you want?
- What's your vision for your life?

You wouldn't leave on a road trip without your GPS or map and for the same reason we don't get on a plane without a flight plan or destination airport. Business owners and entrepreneurs especially need clear goals and objectives, maybe even more so than the average nine-to-five Joe. While many of the business owners I've consulted have some measure of vision and clarity for their lives it's almost always an incomplete picture. You can't build your life on an ambiguous conglomeration of your family's expectations, the rules of society or pure fantasy. That's why determining a baseline is so important.

Just like any journey you need to know where you are, what your resources are and where you are going. If any of those three things are obscure the journey is doomed from the start.

The next exercise, will bring you greater clarity on where you are and what you want.

THE *LIFE CIRCLE EXERCISE*

10 Different Life Domains
- Money & Finances
- Partner & Love
- Work & Career
- Friends & Family
- Fun & Recreation
- Growth & Learning
- Spirituality & Connectedness
- Legacy & Impact
- Health & Fitness
- Community & Environment
    It's time to act. Looking at the different domains bust out your journal and write a few sentences about each.

The questions below should get you started, but don't cheat yourself by doing the minimum. And DON'T skip this step. You bought the book—so do the work and get your money's worth.

- What do I like about this area of my life and why?
- What is bothering me in this area and why?
- What do I wish was different/improved in this area and why?

When your done writing out your thoughts refer to the chart below. Determine your level satisfaction for each individual domain in the circle by rating them on a scale from 1-10. One being not satisfied at all, and ten being highly satisfied with absolutely no room for improvement. If you rate any of your domains with a ten, they need to be absolutely incredible, like fireworks and ecstasy all day long, alright?

Make sure to rate them as they currently are, not on what you hope they will be soon. Remember that this is not a measurement of your contentedness. We can learn to be content with much less than what truly satisfies us. When you're done mark the lines in each domain with your personal rating and connect the dots. The circle represents your overall satisfaction in life.

Life Circle

When we first introduced Cindy to the Life Circle exercise, she assumed that the Circle would say she needed to put more time into her marriage and children because she was a young mom and that's what society says to young moms.

When she finished her circle, she was shocked. You see, she was very satisfied with her marriage and family but extremely dissatisfied with her education and career. A truth she had never even admitted to herself. She needed to make time for her work and career domain. It took a few weeks and some problem solving but she was able to invest more time and energy into her freelancing writing career and create a blog.

Making these changes brought her joy and improved every area of her life including her time with her husband and children.

Finding Values

Moving forward let's identify some of your values. Values are a part of determining your baseline because they define who you are and who you are not. They also affirm what you want and what you don't want.

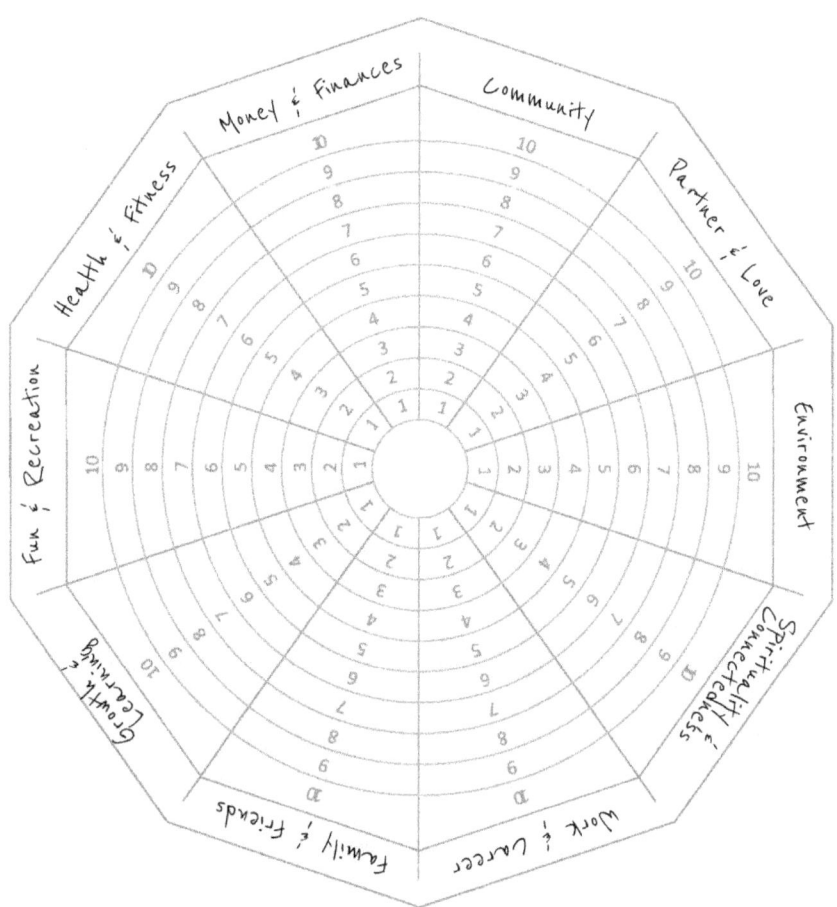

Knowing your values will help you to avoid choices that aren't authentic to your personality and morals.

Every domain in your Life Circle will have its own unique set of values. What you love about your Work and Career will usually be very different from what you value in your Partner and Love domain or what renews and revitalizes you in your Spirituality and Connectedness.

Choose one domain you want to improve your sense of satisfaction in. Next you'll find a list of values to choose from. Select and match up at least 5 values and write them out on the notes page provided at the end of the chapter.

Values List

Acceptance I Achievement I Advancement I Promotion I Adventure I Affection I Altruism I Arts I Awareness I Beauty I Challenge I Change I Community I Compassion I Competence I Competition I Completion I Connectedness I Cooperation I Collaboration I Country I Creativity I Decisiveness I Democracy I Design I Discoveryl Diversity I Environmental I Awareness I Economic I Security I Education I Effectiveness I Efficiency I Elegance I Entertainment I Enlightenment I Equality I Ethics I Excellence I Excitement I Experiment I Expertise I Fairness I Fame I Family I Happiness I Fast Pacel Freedom I Friendship I Fun I Grace I Growth I Harmony I Healthl Helping Others I Helping Society I Honesty I Humor I Imaginationl Improvement I Independencel Influencing I Others I Inner Harmony I Inspiration I Integrity I Intellect I Involvement I Knowledge I Leadership I Learning I Loyalty I Magnificence I Making a Differencel Mastery I Meaningful Work I Ministering I Money I Morality I Mystery I Nature I Openness I Originality I Order I Peace I Personal Development I Personal Expression I Planning I Play I Pleasure I Powerl Privacy I Purity I Quality I Radiance I Recognition I Relationships I Religion IReputation I Responsibility I Accountability I Risk I Safety & Security I Self-Respect ISensibility I Sensuality I Serenity I Service I Sexuality I Sophistication I Spark I Speculation I Spirituality I Stabilityl Status I Success I Teaching I Tenderness I Thrill I Unity I Variety I Wealth I Winning I Wisdom

We wholeheartedly recommend posting your values where you will see them every day. It will help you stay focused on what truly matters to you and it will keep you energized and inspired.

You've got your baseline pretty well-handled now, but, before we move on let's take some time and write out one goal for your focus domain based on any of your 5 chosen values.

We call this process value-alignment. Put these value words in your memory bank for future reference. As you're going throughout your day ask yourself,

"Is how I am doing this, lining-up with my core values?"

Goals are fixed locations like a finish line, but value-alignments are more fluid and flexible like a course correction. Goals do not always align with values, but value-alignment will always result in met goals.

Let me give you a couple hypotheticals:

In Money and Finances, you could value success, status, risk, incentive, and competition.

A goal based on those values could be... Increasing sales by ten percent and qualifying for your company's flagship cruise... Or breaking into seven figures a year and buying a brand-new Porche.

Or again in Money and Finances, you could value security, peace, mastery, independence, and wisdom.

A goal based on those values would be vastly different. It may look more like... Allocating more of your income to an IRA... Or creating a financial plan that can help you grow your nest egg.

I'll give one more for Money and Finances, and then you can get going on your goal. Let's say that a person values altruism, equality, helping society, making a difference and ministering.

A goal based on those values could look like... Giving to local or international charities. Running a non-profit in an area you're passionate about.

Now to be fair, the examples I gave were a little stereotyped. But hopefully it gave you an idea how our values help to shape meaningful goals for us as individuals. Go ahead and write out your goal in one sentence. Use your goal to begin identifying your root motivations.

VALUES LIST

_____

_____

_____

_____

_____

_____

_____

_____

_____

_____

_____

_____

_____

_____

_____

_____

_____

_____

_____

_____

Biological

The Funnel

Social

Four

Psychological

Spiritual

Super
Powers

Not-To-
Do List

ENTIRE

4 st

Hone
Strengths

Step 2
Identifying Root Motivations

7 LEVELS

"If you're doing something you love, you are more likely to put your all into it and that generally equates to making money."
—Warren Buffet

Why do some marketing campaigns bomb and others exceed expectations? Why do certain businesses develop followings while others struggle to create a customer base?

Steve Jobs may have had his flaws, but he was able to develop a cult-following for a computer and technology company. I couldn't think of a drier, less interesting subject than computer programming and technology, and yet people who aren't big technology buffs absolutely rave about their Macs and iPhones. They go out in droves to buy the new products. Somehow Jobs was able to create a movement, a mob-following. How did he do it?

Jobs wanted to change the world by giving creative people the tools they needed to accomplish the work they loved. His motivation, clearly communicated, worked wonders because people don't buy things—emotions do.

Myth-Busted

A highly believed MYTH is that people need to be motivated.

It's a complete lie.

People are already motivated. You're motivated, I'm motivated—we are all motivated!!! Motivation is just a fancy word for **emotion** making it literally the furthest thing from rational thought in the universe. No amount of information can motivate you. No amount of education, or intellect can motivate you.

I want you to think back to something you did that was really stupid. Not just an ooops, or a that was dumb—but something you did that was s-t-u-p-i-d. Maybe it was a bad relationship, a traffic violation or an unfortunate tattoo it doesn't matter as long as you knew it was a bad idea before you did it and you did it anyway. That means that knowledge, information, intellect and rational thinking were not on-board with the stupid thing, right? Alright then—there's your proof. Motivation doesn't stem from logic. Why, because emotion trumps information all day long!

So, if you've ever done anything stupid, and trust me we all have, then, motivation is not your problem. Pretending your emotions aren't moving you is what's cutting you off at the knees.

The good news I want you to hear is that you don't lack motivation. You don't have to 'get motivated' because you have it in spades my friend. I'm about to show you how to find and wield your root motivations to defeat your setbacks and excuses once and for all.

MAMA BEAR

Let's say we both know a lady named Paula. Now, Paula is a sweet, gentle, soft-spoken person. She makes the world's best Snickerdoodle cookies and plays board games with her kids. For fun she knits sweaters for homeless kittens. She is literally the nicest—sweetest—kindest person of all time!

Just the other day Paula was sitting on a park bench texting her husband when a bear rambled out of the bushes. Out of nowhere, Paula threw her iPhone away and tackled that bear, pummeling it with the strength of ten men. She had it pinned-down in a choke hold when the Department of Wildlife finally arrived and hit it with a tranquilizer dart.

What got into Paula?
Why did she attack the bear?

Well, what I didn't tell you is that the bear had tried to grab Paula's newborn baby right out of the stroller. In the light of that information doesn't Paula's reaction suddenly make a ton of sense?

Paula attacked because she had a deep and motivating WHY. The bear was a threat to something she greatly valued, her child.

Can you think of anything you value that much?
Your kids? Your Spouse? Your friends?

Now, think about it, what if the bear had scratched Paula's car instead? I doubt she would have put herself in danger to protect it. Scratched paint just isn't that big of a deal compared to human life. She wouldn't have even thrown her phone either—I mean c'mon they're expensive. No—she would have backed away slowly, probably taking some sweet pictures to post on social media.

Why?

Because the value she placed on her car was far less than the value she placed on her child.

Fast forward a bit. Let's say that videos of her tackling the bear go mega-viral. Paula is featured on the nightly news as the 'Mama Bear' and even gets paid to endorse some bear spray. Then she's offered a sweet job doing commercials for "extreme-outdoorsmen-products", making her a nice chunk of change. Her Instagram blew up. Her TED talk hit one million views in its first week. It was nuts.

Did she fight the bear to get famous? HECK NO!

Your motivation in life has to be bigger than becoming well-known, independently wealthy or having more free time!!!

I hear it all the time. Everyone is "going into business to have financial freedom." That's a wimpy WHY. It's the equivalent of the bear scratching your car. You might not like it, but can live with scratched paint.

To have a meaningful, UNSTOPPABLE WHY you need to have a endangered baby. Not literally, thank God, but you need more than a nice idea as a reason to win. You need a WHY BABY, and it needs to be something that you cannot live without.

Here's a great litmus test: If you can walk away from your WHY BABY then it isn't a WHY BABY. It's just an ideal, or a great idea, it may be something that you really love but it's not a WHY BABY. Paula would never have been okay with losing her baby. It could have been two bears and she wouldn't have backed down. In fact, you could've thrown three bears and a land roaming great white shark at her and she would never have given up. That's the kind of motivation we need to unearth in this second step.

In Step One, you've determined your baseline. You know who you are and what you want. Now we're going to find out what moves you. Your Why-Baby is pure emotion—the most motivating, inspirational thing in life. That's why successful businesses focus their marketing campaigns on emotions, not intellect. If a marketer can touch on your deepest motivations and offer a solution, it's over. You're going to find the money—because no matter what,

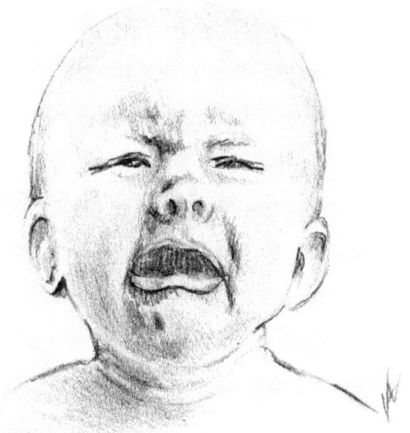

"Why-Baby will get, what Why-Baby wants."

This next 7 Levels exercise, will give you the tools to develop and unearth your deepest motivations. My wife and I discovered this exercise in Dean Graziosi's book, *Millionaire Success Habits*. It was revolutionary to both of us, so of course we built a modified version of it for our clients. It is by far our most impactful exercise.

Trust and Honesty

Fair Warning: This exercise can take an emotional toll. You will need someone you can trust and be completely honest with to help facilitate this exercise. Pick someone that you're okay being real and vulnerable with.

7 Levels is designed to save you 25 years of heartache in about 45 to 90 minutes. To do that it uses some serious brain hacks. Before we get started let me sum up what your brain will be doing in 7 Levels, so you have an idea what to expect.

This is Your Brain...

Most adults spend a vast majority of their brain power in the front-outer portion of their head, the neocortex. This is where logic, common sense, and rational thought abound, and it is definitely not where your Why-Baby lives. Remember logic, and information doesn't motivate—but emotion does. That's why we do stupid things. Remember emotion trumps rational thinking all day long.

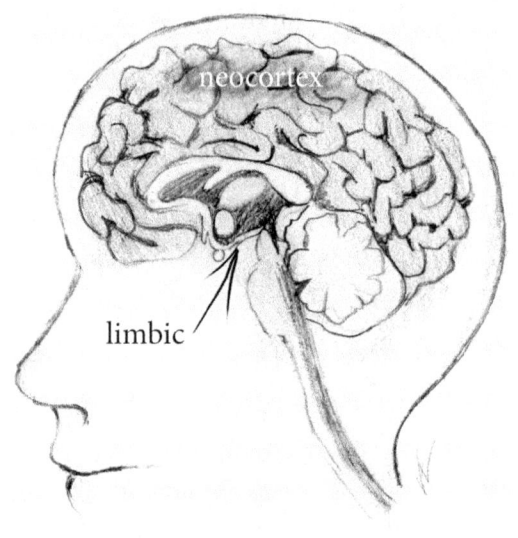

Motivation is in the limbic system right smack dab in the center of your head. It's where we process feelings, and associate meaning to memories and situations. It's also the main hub of our fight or flight stress response.

If you want to triumph in your business or your life you will need powerful motivation. That means moving past the logical responses of our neocortex and getting a hold of the raw emotional answers in our limbic system. That's how you'll find motivation that defies logic and have yourself a WHY BABY!

Think back to Paula, our mama bear. She was absolutely in the throes of a limbic system response when she tackled that bear. There is no way her neocortex was on board with that decision! No sane, intelligent woman could rationalize taking on a grizzly. She logically knew that fighting a bear was a really bad idea but her limbic system made the order and...

BOOM!!! Motivation despite logic!!!

That's what 7 Levels will help you find by helping your brain make the shift from logical to emotional—from your neocortex to your limbic system. It can be a bit of a struggle, so I'll cover more on how to navigate this shift after I explain the exercise itself.

7 LEVELS EXERCISE

Grab your facilitating friend and start by getting into a relaxed state. I recommend recording the exercise and taking some time to journal about your discoveries soon after you finish. It'll give you something to come back to.

You can use the template in the Unstoppable Blueprint Workbook or a blank sheet of paper but let your friend do the writing, so you can focus.

Start by writing out your goal from the end of Step One chapter notes.

For illustration I'm going to use one based in the Health and Fitness domain:

"I want to lose ten pounds, so I can feel strong and have more energy."

Your assistant will ask:

"Why is losing ten pounds to feel strong and have more energy important to you?" or they could say a variation like, "What about losing ten pounds to feel strong and have more energy is important to you right now?"

A common response could be:

"Well, I'm pre-diabetic and I want to prevent diabetes."

That is your level one answer. Your friend will write it down and then repeat back your beginning statement and ask why your level one answer is important to you. It'll look something like this:

"So, you said that you want to lose ten pounds and that it was important to you because you want to prevent diabetes and improve your health. Why do you think preventing diabetes and improving your health is important to you?"

Your next answer is level two. Your friend will write it down and then review your original goal, your level one and then ask you why your level two is important to you. Do you see the pattern?

The process repeats all the way down to the seventh level, or answer. With each answer you go deeper into what really motivates you.

Here's the completed example without the facilitator's repetitions:

- "I want to lose ten pounds, so I can feel strong and have more energy."
- "Well, I'm pre-diabetic and I want to prevent diabetes."
- "I want to live a long, healthy life."
- "I want to be there for my grandchildren."
- "I want them to remember me well."
- "I want to love and support them."
- "I want my family, my legacy to be healthy, and happy."
- "I want to be significant"

Can you see how the answers become more emotional and less logical the further down the list we go? That's the brain shifting from the neocortex to the limbic system.

The drive for significance and legacy is much more powerful than our drive to just lose weight.

I must have significance, or my life feels like a waste. At the same time losing weight would be nice, but I can live with love-handles if I have to.

The original statement about losing weight, compared to the seventh level's, "need for significance," is the difference between Paula (our mama bear), dealing with scratched paint or a stolen baby.

This is Hard!

It seems simple enough, but we've had this one exercise take up to two hours with clients that really struggled to make the shift from logic to emotion.

I'll be honest guys, this exercise can be tough, especially if you're not an emotional person. I get it. I'm not all that "touchy-feely" either but if you're having a really hard time it could be that you have some unconnected stuff from your past. Typically, it's neglect, abuse, abandonment, or harsh internal messaging. If that's you, then here's how you get past the brain shift and find your root motivation. Trust me it's in there.

Close your eyes and acknowledge the resistance you're feeling. Stay relaxed and sit with the question. The answers will come, and the key is acceptance. Your job is to accept whatever feelings come up without judgment. Remember that feelings aren't wrong or right; good or bad. Feelings are helpful indicators of our met and unmet needs.

I once had an Oldsmobile that went through oil by the case. When the oil light came on it was not a good light or a bad light. It was a helpful notification that I'd forgotten to fill my oil. Just like that light, any feelings you get while working through this exercise are just helpful messengers—not good or bad.

Lost in Translation

So, you're relaxed, you're accepting your feelings but you're still struggling. Another potential roadblock is that the limbic system communicates in emotions, pictures and memories—not words. I recommend that you try to describe what you're experiencing and ask your friend to help you wrap language around it.

A helpful tip is to pay attention to your body. If you begin to sense tightness, heaviness, stress or a 'bad' feeling that's an indication of strong emotions. The same is true for happy, joyful feelings which tend to feel warm and light. Sit with the feelings and breathe until your brain can put it into words.

Work down the levels by following the strongest emotions. If you have a couple answers on a level and you're not sure which one to go with, then write them both down and follow the one with the strongest emotional pull—an I want, or aversion—an I don't want. A strong aversion is important because, your limbic system is screaming, "Danger!" It's important to know where that comes from for you. Difficult feelings come from false belief patterns, trauma and abuse and that can take some time to unravel.

A lot of us are motivated to avoid the pain we experienced as children. If you find that your answers are looking too negative don't worry. Just write them down and give them room to breathe. Ask yourself what you want to gain, not avoid. Typically, it's what was denied you; safety, attention, value, support, significance, freedom, control, respect, and/or love.

Why Do You Love Your Wife?

I'll give you another example before we move on. When someone asks me why I love my wife my neocortex says, "I love her, because I love her. Isn't it obvious? She's great. She's beautiful. She's helpful."

Can you see how those logical answers hardly scratch the surface of the deep emotional connection I share with my wife? They are also not super strong motivation to stay married when times get tough.

But ask the same question to my limbic system and you'll get, "Loving my wife feels like waking up to a beautiful sunrise every day" and "I don't know why but I smell autumn leaves and apple cider." Or "When she's happy it feels like Christmas and I can't help but smile." Can you feel the difference? In these you can see my need for joy, variety and comfort is met.

Now let's say hypothetically that some negative beliefs are motivating my relationship with my wife. I could bring up painful memories of neglect or betrayal and come out like, "I love my wife because she would never hurt me like my mother did," or "She gives me the respect I never got from my Dad." "Because not loving my wife means I'm a failure." In this case I would be looking for respect, safety, trust, and reassurance.

Remember to give any negative motivations time and acceptance. They are your feelings and deserve your respect. Honor them.

Wrap it Up

Your 7th Level should feel pretty emotional. It's your heartbeat, everything that moves you, and when you can communicate it effectively it's going to trigger something emotional, and deep in others. This all started by getting that baseline in the Life Circle and owning your values in just one domain. Now you've identified your root motivation that directly influences that single life domain. By defining your motivations and using them as a base to operate from, you're going to have a huge emotional impact on the people you interact with, no matter which domain you start with.

I recommend doing this entire process once a month with every life domain in your Life Circle. It will absolutely change your life. The even better news is that as you continue to master the 7 Levels, you can unearth your motives in any area of your life in a matter of minutes. So, do the work and you'll save yourself a mid-life crisis, sharpen your focus and have the tools to structure an incredible fulfilled future.

Let me tell you about Richard. Richard is a successful business owner, coach, and client who had a crystal-clear picture of his future. His children were soon to graduate high school with honors, and he planned to pay their way through university. He was also working to sell his home and move to a more expensive city near their chosen schools. He had some ambitious financial goals and was on track to meet them ahead of schedule. He was already crushing it. So much so, that I, (Rachel) wondered if 7 Levels would benefit him much at all. As we dug a little deeper and Richard's brain made the leap from logic to emotion, a very powerful truth emerged from his childhood.

Richard's father, while being a faithful and generous provider, was emotionally unavailable to his children and wife. Richard sat with this awareness for some time considering how his father's aloof and unconnected relationship could be affecting his deepest motivations decades later. He realized that his goals weren't just financial. Instead they were relational. He realized that all his efforts to provide for his wife and children were his way of working to create healthy emotional connection with them. This desire for healthy connection was what had been moving him all along but now that he was fully aware of it, he could reposition himself to intentionally build connection. He refocused his goals on meaningful connection and immediately felt a surge of motivation and rejuvenation in his life and business.

AFFIRMATIONS

As a special bonus before we move on, I'd like to show you how to turn your 7 Levels discoveries into positive affirmations. Affirmations you can read in the morning, before bed, during difficult times or as a healthy motivator before an important meeting.

It is life changing.

The example below is pulled from the weight loss example earlier in this chapter. Each level of the exercise is morphed into a positive I statement.

- I am strong and bursting with youthful energy.
- I am overcoming type 2 diabetes every day. I make healthy choices moving me closer to a healthier blood sugar level.
- I'm healthy and full of life and longevity.
- I am present and supportive of all my children and grandchildren.
- Every day I make meaningful memories with my family that they will cherish long after I'm gone.
- I am a pillar of love and support to my children and grandchildren.
- I am creating a lasting legacy.
- I am significant.

7 LEVELS

_____

_____

_____

_____

_____

_____

_____

_____

_____

_____

_____

_____

_____

_____

_____

_____

_____

_____

_____

_____

_____

_____

_____

_____

_____

_____

_____

AFFIRMATIONS

_____

_____

_____

_____

_____

_____

_____

_____

_____

_____

_____

_____

_____

_____

_____

_____

_____

_____

_____

_____

_____

_____

THE PERFECT DAY

"Your time is limited, so don't waste it living someone else's life. Don't be trapped by dogma – which is living with the results of other people's thinking. Don't let the noise of other's opinions drown out your own inner voice. And most important, have the courage to follow your heart and intuition. They somehow already know what you truly want to become.
Everything else is secondary."
– Steve Jobs

Owning your deepest motivations, like you just did in the 7 Levels exercise and then continually affirming them is like throwing lighter fluid on a bonfire.

It creates MASSIVE MOTIVATION!!! But throwing gas on a fire isn't any good if there aren't any logs to sustain it long-term. After 7 Levels we find ourselves filled with inspiration and new vigor ready to rock-and-roll, but where do we take that energy?

All too often as entrepreneurs we look to other already successful entrepreneurs to figure out what we should be doing and copy them. We follow their every move instead of looking at our own unique desires and gifts. When we build our businesses entirely from someone else's formula then we've foolishly invested in building the business and life of another man's dreams. Because it was never our dream it becomes our prison.

That's why the last two steps so important. In Step One, Determining Your Baseline, got you reflecting about where you are in life and what you value. Your work on the exercises supply a powerful WHY BABY that will inspire you to take on the "bears" of adversity. Now we're going to get even clearer on where you want to go with the Perfect Day. But first, listen to Sarah's story...

A Little Slice of Heaven

In his book, *The E Myth*, Michael Gerber shares about an entrepreneur three years into her venture named Sarah.

Sarah owns and operates a well-loved pie bakery. Her daily routine begins with waking at 2:00am, baking pies at the bakery from 3am until opening the doors at 7am. Then she works all day, and takes care of all the other operations required like accounting, ordering, taxes, marketing, etc... She gets done around 6 or 7:00pm to go home and take care of her family until falling into bed around 10pm to get up and do it all over again the following day. Seven days a week.

In the end, Sarah hates pies, baking, and she dreads opening her bakery every morning because her work never ends. I doubt that Sarah went into business to be exhausted and hate pies. I'll bet that in her head this bakery would be a little slice of heaven. But that wasn't what she was living. She was the best pie-maker in the county. All her friends told her to go into business, so she did. Everyone said that she'd be wildly successful, and, in a way, she was. But she was also exhausted and miserable.

If we're not careful we can end up like Sarah, doing what we think we should and hating it. The

Perfect Day will give a picture of your best possible outcome so you can avoid getting into a business you'll hate or figure out what ways to delegate in a business you wish you didn't hate.

THE PERFECT DAY

I want you to imagine a day with no limitations. No requirements. No obligations. A day where you choose; do whatever, see whomever and go wherever you want. A day where you are completely, authentically yourself.

These are the basic parameters of the Perfect Day, an exercise we use when coaching clients. You're going to write at least a page on your Perfect Day from start to finish. From when you get out of bed to when you get back in.

The goal of this is self-discovery, and trajectory—this exercise will show you where you really want to go. But it won't work if you don't have fun so it's necessary that you approach it playfully.

Write out everything—yes, everything you ever wanted for your life, but couldn't have because you were limited by time, money or motivation. This is not what you should do, not what your spouse, kids or friends want you to do. There are no obligations and no strings attached. For once it's absolutely all about YOU. It's everything you ever wanted written down in one Perfect Day.

We encourage our clients to spend time on this. Dream a little. Get creative. What makes you feel alive, excited and passionate? Make sure it makes your day brighter and creates anticipation every step of the way.

The only things you can't have are things you should do; responsibilities, obligations, or requirements whatsoever—if you don't want to eat your vegetables then don't!

Write everything out and remember there are no right or wrong answers.

Our Perfect Days

When my wife, Rachel, did her Perfect Day, she woke up in a historic house on the beach in a bed with soft, cool sheets. She puts her feet down onto a luxurious sheepskin rug and instantly the perfect cup of coffee appears in a beautiful hand-thrown mug. As she sips her drink, she watches the sun rise. Comfortable and quiet she can hear the gentle sound of the waves in the background, and the seagulls calling. She can smell the salty sea air through the open window. All her favorite writing supplies are on the desk facing the ocean where she writes without interruption until she's ready to head out for breakfast with me and the kids. And then we all go hiking and playing on the beach as a family.

What does this tell us? To put it simply my wife wants alone time, comfort, peace, and tactile luxury. She wants to write uninterrupted. Notice her attention to the feel of the fabrics, her cup, the scents and sounds. Sensory luxury is important to her and for her to be happy and fulfilled she must build peace and luxury into her day. And we got that from just her first paragraph! Now, let's look at Stephen's.

My Perfect Day starts with a partying mob rushing into my room chanting, "(Stephen), (Stephen), Stephen!" They pull me out of bed, put me on their shoulders and, shout, "Hooray!" I can tell that these people are my biggest fans. My whole day is packed with excitement, competition and adventure. We're heading off to see my favorite European soccer teams, and later that day I'm speaking at a conference followed by a high-profile business meeting. My friends and family are cheering me on! Just thinking about it gets me all fired up and excited.

What does that tell us? That I want celebration, appreciation, competition and excitement in my life! The good news is that I don't need a carousing mob to invade my bedroom every morning to get that same feeling in my day.

While what's in your day is important but it's also important to notice what is NOT in your day.

We were working with Colton, a smart, capable business man, who after many years still hadn't launched the internet marketing venture he'd been talking about. When we took him through his Perfect Day, he talked about his love of nature, hunting, drag racing, fixing up collector cars and spending time in the outdoors with his family. Not once in his entire day did, he mention sitting at a computer, making phone calls, or dealing in any way with marketing. In fact, in his entire day he didn't step indoors at all. The only technology he mentioned was a fully equipped and immaculately clean machine shop.

Now think about that for a second. Would internet marketing have fulfilled this man? Maybe, but probably not in the long term. This exercise gave our friend a major clue why he had been so hesitant to launch his online business. It was a smart business, but he wasn't passionate about it. This exercise alone saved him from the heartache and financial cost of what could have been a failed business. Or even worse, a successful business he would have hated.

Now, think back to Sara, the pie lady. Her bakery took a ton of time to run and required her to do a lot of different tasks. I'll bet that she didn't think owning a bakery was going to be much more than baking pies before she got started. If she had done a Perfect Day, she would have had an idea which activities would have brought her joy, and which would give her a migraine. Then she could have delegated those less than desirable tasks away. I'll talk more about delegation in the next chapter. For now, I want you to go ahead and get started on your Perfect Day. Below you'll find a list of questions to get the ball rolling.

Questions to Get You Started on Your Perfect Day.

Where do you wake up?

What would you do if you didn't need a job to pay your bills?

What wakes you up?

What do you do first?

What do you eat for breakfast, lunch & dinner and who cooked it?

Do you stay indoors, or do you go outside?

Are the tasks you do physical, mental or social?

What are you wearing?

What places do you visit?
What kind of people are you spending time with it?
Are work people there?
What is your connection to your Creator?
Are you talking to God?
What emotions do you feel?
How does your body feel?
What's your energy level?
Where do you go to rest and relax?
What you see, what do you hear, what do you smell, what do you touch and taste?
Where is your spouse/significant other?
Do you see your children?
Where is your extended family?
What do you travel in?

Once you're done, keep your finished copy and look at it again in a few days. You may end up tweaking, changing, adding or taking away. That's okay. This is your day it can change with you. I (Stephen), was recently revisiting my Perfect Day when I realized how much I valued being in nature and fishing. I had to ask myself why I wasn't fishing more. It is a useful tool to keep you accountable to your own values and goals. We must be detailed and intentional as we translate our Perfect Day into our lives. Get clear about what you love and enjoy and build it into your life.

"The only way to do great work, is to love what you do."
–Steve Jobs

Steve Jobs was highly motivated and fulfilled by his work. If you had to guess, how close do you think Jobs' life was to his Perfect Day?

I think pretty darn close and here's why. When Jobs took Pixar public in 1995 his eighty percent share increased in value to around one billion dollars. That's a one with nine zeros folks! Logically Jobs didn't have to continue working—at that point his bills were paid, and he was free to retire and take up snorkeling if he wanted.

When he was invited to return and resuscitate a nearly bankrupt Apple he said yes. He really didn't have to, but he did. Jobs loved his work and believed in it. He built his businesses to reflect his deepest motivations. He was successful because he crafted his life in the image of his Perfect Day every day. The same could be said of any wholehearted, *The Unstoppable Entrepreneur*.

The same could be said of you.

But only if you will take this message to heart. You are unique. Your dreams and desires are important. You matter. You can base your life, your family and your business on your Perfect Day, making it the lens through which you make all your decisions. Then with every choice you can build the life and business of your dreams.

MY PERFECT DAY

_____

_____

_____

_____

_____

_____

_____

_____

_____

_____

_____

_____

_____

_____

_____

_____

_____

_____

_____

_____

_____

_____

_____

_____

_____

_____

_____

_____

_____

_____

_____

_____

_____

_____

_____

_____

_____

_____

_____

_____

_____

_____

_____

_____

_____

_____

_____

_____

_____

_____

_____

Biological

The Funnel

Social

Psychological

Four

Spiritual

Super
Powers

Not-To-
Do List

uns
ENTIRE

4 st

Hone
Strengths

Step 3
Honing Your Strengths

Determine a
Baseline

Value
Alignment

Life Circle

Identify Root
Motives

7 Levels

process

HIDDEN SUPER POWERS

"A computer once beat me at chess, but it was no match for me at kick boxing." – **Emo Philips**

I would've loved to have been a fly on the wall the day Warren Buffet and Bill Gates first met.

According to Buffet their meeting was set up by their wives who had met a few times at charitable functions. In their first meeting Warren Buffet says he was sitting in his home office when Bill Gates walked up and handed him a piece of paper saying, "I want you to write down the one word that defines your success, and life. While you do that, I'll write down the one word that defines mine and then we'll compare."

The one word that they both wrote down was focus.

Focus

Think of all the things that you do in a day that are a definite weakness for you. How much time do those tasks take up? What if, like magic, those tasks were handled by someone else? Wouldn't it be wonderful? How different would your life be? How much more could you accomplish if you solely focused on your strengths?

In the last three chapters we worked hard to determine your baseline, and discover your root motivations with 7 levels and the Perfect Day. Now it's time to see what you've got under the hood. It's time to hone your strengths. We're going to take a note from Gates and Buffet and really focus in on what you should be focusing on.

Let's get down to brass tacks and start fleshing these values and motivations into reality, by inventorying the best tools at your disposal.

You Got the Skills to Pay the Bills

"Never love anyone who treats you like your ordinary." – **Oscar Wilde**

WHAT ARE YOUR SUPERPOWERS?

You may already know your strengths, but have you ever really thought about what your SUPERPOWERS are? I'm not talking x-ray vision or super strength although both sound good to me. I mean your unique abilities? Often, we find that our clients don't notice or see the value in their innate gifts. Either they assume everyone has their super power or that their strength isn't valuable.

For instance, my wife has the unique gift of putting strangers at ease. We've been late to school, church, weddings, family events, sports, you name it—all because people feel so safe and at ease with her that they open up about very personal issues. I mean complete strangers. I'll come up to the checkout in a hurry and find the cashier crying on her shoulder about their struggle with addiction, or an abusive spouse. When I say life story I mean, "Their... Entire... Life... Story...". She's so focused on the person she's talking to that she hardly notices me standing there. It's an incredible gift and what amazes me the most is that her whole life my wife never once thought it was special, or even a gift.

She actually believed that anybody could get a complete stranger to tell them the most vulnerable parts of their life story in less than two minutes.

We all have innate gifts that we think are no big deal. I'm going to help you identify them and put them to good use.

Put Me in Coach

A lot of times we assume that our gifts are all encompassing and follow our passions—yeah no. My wife is good with strangers, but she is drained by meeting a lot of new people every day. After a few hours of meet and greet she is exhausted.

I'm a gifted athlete, sports and coordination come easily to me. I've always had a knack for it. I love soccer and I still play with some top-level soccer players. Last year I thought it would be cool to coach my 7-year-old son's soccer team. I watch soccer, play soccer, and am passionate about soccer. It turns out, that I am also a not so-awesome soccer coach for 7-year-old boys.

I never thought 7-year-olds could make me cry. I don't even have words for how truly horrible it was. It was that bad. Even though the

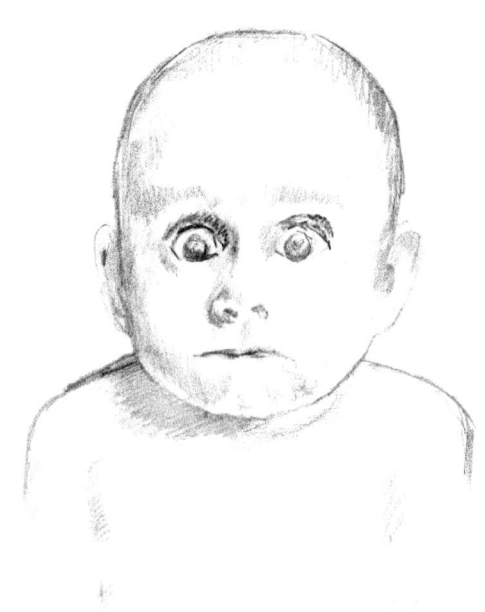

coaching had to do with one of my major passions it was still out of my wheel house. Passion does not equal ability. When it comes to SUPERPOWERS it's important to be very specific. "I'm good at soccer", doesn't cut it. "I'm good at playing center-back or sweeper in the 30-year-old and up soccer league" is better. You follow?

Grab out some paper or a white board and let's do an exercise that will help you to see what's unique and special about you. Try to be more specific than "I'm good at soccer."

You can involve your spouse, kids, family, and friends if you'd like, but limit it to only those who will give you an honest opinion. Don't invite mean people. I want you to brainstorm a list of at least 10 items on paper or white board. Anything fun, cool or unique about you. Everything you excel at is important even if you fail to see how it's relevant.

Nobody Likes Me Everybody Hates Me

If you don't have an overflow of supportive friends and family willing to brainstorm this out with you, I can offer you a couple solutions. The first is a powerful hack I learned from Barbara Sher's book *WishCraft*. When you can't find the support you need, you can build your own Fanclub.

Fanclub 101

All you need to do is think of some actors, historical, figures, authors, or political figures that you admire and relate to. Write down five to ten names. It could be anyone, dead or alive and at any age. Some popular choices are Albert Einstein, Taylor Swift, Will Smith, Abraham Lincoln, Martin Luther King Jr., Steve Carell—once again there are no limits. You can even choose fictitious characters like Harry Potter, Gandalf, or Sherlock Holmes. All that matters are that you admire and relate to them.

Here's how this works. These people are now your closest friends and they all admire and respect you tremendously. In this exercise you need to imagine that you are covertly witnessing a reporter interview these famous five to ten people one at a time.

The reporter asks each one the questions below and all you have to do is imagine their responses and write them down.

- *What drew you toward (insert your name here)?*
- *What is the secret to (insert your name here) success?*
- *What makes (insert your name here) special to you?*
- *What do you love about (insert your name here)?*

I chose Thor of Asgard, Bear Grylls, Kevin Hart, Jim Gaffigan, Peter the Apostle, and Joel Osteen because he's always smiling and turning everything into a positive. My wife had JK Rowling, Jane Austin, Morgan Freeman, Sean Connery, Chip & Joanna Gaines, and a songwriter from Australia.

This exercise will give you a glimpse of what you hope others see in you. Add what you find to your white board top twenty and we'll get moving on.

The second solution I can recommend as you identify your strengths is the mighty personality test!

There are two types of people. Those who love personality tests and those who have a life and see little to no value in them. I was the latter until my wife, after ten years of trying, finally prevailed against me. Now,

I'm a believer and have no life. Despite my initial disbelief I found my results to be insightful and helpful.

The two "mighty personality tests" we use with our clients are:

- **The Myers-Briggs Personality Test**, also known as the **16 Personality Test** that can be found for free at https://*www.16personalities.com/personality-types*

and

- **The DISC Test** also very popular and available for free available at *https://www.tonyrobbins.com/disc*

Both tests take less than twenty minutes and will give you the option to have your results emailed to you. As you review your results pay special attention to your strengths and add them to your list of potential SUPERPOWERS.

Mental Health Quick Side Note:

If you have been diagnosed or suspect that you have ADHD, ADD, OCD, depression, or anxiety don't be too quick to list your mental health challenge as a deficit. Some of the most brilliant and influential people throughout history struggled with mental illness and were able to use the gift within their struggle to succeed where others failed.

I believe that those who struggle with mental health can withstand pressure from without because they have had to overcome intense pressure from within. They also tend to be more empathetic and better communicators.

What if your mental health issue is somehow a gift or an ability specific to your unique brain? Don't discount yourself. Instead, find the positive angle in your mental health challenge and use it to your advantage. Who knows? It could be a superpower.

BULLS-EYE

I want you to draw a bulls-eye on a large piece of paper, take your group brain storm and/or your Fanclub notes and start placing your strengths on your bullseye. The center bullseye is for SUPERPOWERS. Things you do better than anybody you know in real life. Things you love. Things you wish you could do instead of working your 9-5. Things that come naturally to you, that you enjoy learning about and growing in. These are the things you chose to do in your spare time.

The middle ring will be the things you do better than most people with less effort. Things you enjoy and are efficient at.

The outer ring will be the things your pretty good at and you don't mind doing on a regular basis. These could also be something you're not good at but still enjoy.

If any of the strengths you have left do not fit any of the above criteria then they've missed the target, but no worries we will need them for the next exercise.

Leaky Pipes

Now, we're going to create a Not-To-Do-List. Yes, I want you to write out a list of things you suck at but first I want to tell you why outdoor plumbing is at the top of my list.

A few years ago, I owned a home with a pool. One day the pump on said pool gave out and I thought that I'd save some money installing the new pump myself. You should know that I'm not super handy. I'm okay, but I'm man enough to admit that outdoor plumbing is not my strong suit. I usually hire out this sort of thing, but this time I felt that the cost of paying for the professional was unreasonable. I mean—how hard could it be? You unplug a couple wires, pop some pipes off and install the new ones. Easy-peazy.

I couldn't have been more wrong. My poor wife and kids endured me losing my religion for four hours because of this stupid pump. Nothing was the right height. The wire colors didn't match. None of the YouTube videos I watched were helpful. I couldn't find the right tools. It was bad. I wasn't a nice guy, but I got that stinking pump installed.

Here's the catch. In the process I damaged the sand filter and one of the pipes that led back to the pool. By the next morning it was apparent by the water flooding my backyard that my pump install had gone sideways.

I got to eat crow and call in the professional anyways. Then, I got to replace the pump I'd just bought and the sand filter, both of which I'd inadvertently damaged. I got to pay for all new piping to replace the pipes I'd cracked. Needless to say, I didn't save any money. I didn't save any time and the quality of my relationships suffered because I was angry over the whole situation for a couple days.

Clearly, I have no business wearing the outdoor-plumber-hat.

I should have stuck to my strengths and left plumbing on my Not-To-Do-List.

Multiple Personalities

Now, I know you've got a million reasons why this won't work running through your brain. You feel like you have to do everything because you can't afford to hire anyone, or no one will do it as well as you do. I get it, really, I do. We've been conditioned, as entrepreneurs, to think we have to conquer the whole world alone.

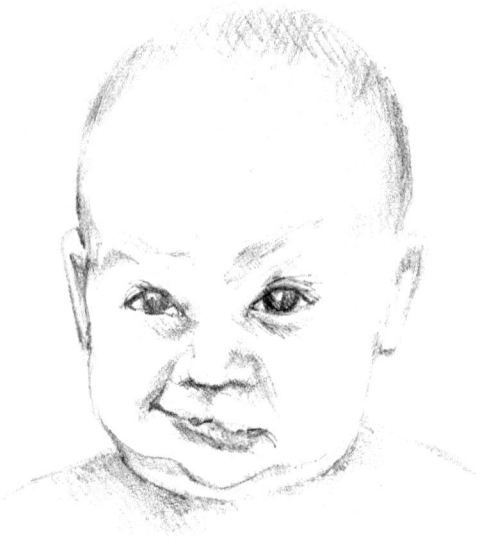

Everybody's trying to be a self-made man. We don't focus on our strengths, we wear way too many hats, and burn out. Sarah, the pie lady, is the perfect example of the entrepreneurial multi-personality disorder we all struggle with from time to time.

We're the marketer, website builder, sales guy, shipping guy, accounting department—you name it. Most of us can't do a good job at half of it, and we're all hopelessly convinced that we're saving ourselves money DIY-ing it.

NEWSFLASH!—we're not!

We lose money doing our own taxes because we aren't CPA's. We lose precious time building our own websites because we don't know html, css, or graphic design and we're having to learn as we go by making costly mistakes. We lose by doing our own marketing because we don't write good copy or understand internet ads or social media marketing.

Despite what you may have thought, your job as an entrepreneur is NOT to just figure everything out. My outdoor plumber story proves that playing Mr. Fix-It is not one of my strengths. You might be thinking,

"C'mon, Stephen. Aren't we supposed to work on our weaknesses?" Okay, let's take that line of thinking one step further and see where it gets us.

Running Against the Wind

Trying to fix a weakness is like running against the wind. But because I'm a good sport let's say that I decided to fix my outdoor plumbing weakness. I would spend hours researching and learning about the outdoor plumbing basics, take a class at a local community college or pay a plumber to teach me. In the end I would have given my precious time and resources to become a crappy plumber. No pun intended.

In the time I spent bettering my outdoor plumbing skills how much money did I make? Zero. How much value did I bring to my home, wife, and kids? Zero. How much did it enrich my experience in life? I'll tell you right now… not one bit. I don't like outdoor plumbing.

Now if I had taken the same amount of time and investment and did something to better one of my strengths, I can guarantee that there would be financial increase. I would have been able to bring value to my home, wife, kids, customers, and employees, and it would have greatly increased my life experience.

Work on your weaknesses and become nominal.
Work on your strengths and be wildly successful.

No matter how hard you work your strongest weakness it is still a weakness.
Likewise, your weakest strength is still a strength.

Don't waste your time running against the wind. When it comes to your strengths you need to go with the flow.

Good or Great?

I know I'm driving this point pretty hard but it's because we as business owners are typically independent, individualistic people and a little set in our ways. When it comes to focusing in on our strengths and delegating our weaknesses you can't be half way in. You've got to be committed to your Not-To-Do-List for it to work. Here's a great example.

Olympians are the greatest athletes in the world, and they are that way because they focus in on what they're great at. They utilize and improve those strengths. You're not going to find Michael Phelps competing in the javelin toss, or singles figure skating. There are even some swim races he didn't participate in. Instead of being a jack of-all-trades Phelps focused on his SUPERPOWERS and ignored what he was only good at. He trained exclusively for the events that he was extraordinary at. It takes great focus and discipline to live in your SUPERPOWERS, but what you are good at will always be a distraction to what you are great at.

What if one of these Olympic level athletes had been pulled aside by a coach, they respected who told them they needed to work on their weaknesses. Maybe they needed to put more effort into their social life, or chess game. If they had followed advice like that, we wouldn't even know their names today. No, they kept their mediocrity on the Not-To-Do-List and their strengths in the forefront to become Olympic level athletes.

Help I've Fallen, & I Can't Get Up

From now on I want you to think of your weaknesses as disabilities. Stop trying to fix them and start accommodating them. Trying to fix your disabilities will only exhaust and frustrate you. For the sake of your business, your family and your health you need to start considering yourself a helpless invalid in your areas of weakness.

Remember those old Life Alert commercials? From now on you're the elderly person that falls and breaks a hip every time you do something outside of your SUPERPOWERS. The Life Alert button is you giving yourself permission to stop wasting your time and energy dragging yourself across the floor. Just say the words, "Help, I've fallen, and I can't get up."

Here's the truth: outsourcing is not a sign of weakness—it's a sign of intelligence.

If you want greatness and health, you have no choice. You must reach out for support, and help. You have incredible SUPERPOWERS, but in the end you're still not Superman. To truly hone your strengths and leverage them to their full potential you need a team of amazing people around you. But first let's get that list of things you're not good at done.

THE NOT-TO-DO LIST

To make your Not-To-Do-List all you have to do is write down all the tasks you are not good at, that take up your time, frustrate and annoy you.

Remember Sarah, the pie lady? She was overwhelmed in her bakery business and needed to find ways to delegate. She might have written down paying the bills or balancing the books, marketing and online order management, taxes and licensing. Whatever it is. If you honestly suck at it and/

or it drives you nuts, then FOR THE LOVE OF PIE just write it down!

Then go back to the top of the list and write in big bold letters— MY NOT-TO-DO LIST!!! Post it right by your desk and stop doing everything on that list as soon as possible.

In the next chapter I'll show you how to maximize your return on your Not-To-Do-List by bringing in the right people with the right incentive-based relationships to increase your productivity, satisfaction and bottom line. Let's build your team.

GOOD AT

_____

_____

_____

_____

_____

_____

_____

_____

_____

_____

_____

_____

_____

_____

_____

_____

_____

_____

_____

_____

_____

_____

_____

_____

_____

_____

GREAT AT

_____

_____

_____

_____

_____

_____

_____

_____

_____

_____

_____

_____

_____

_____

_____

_____

_____

_____

_____

_____

_____

_____

_____

SUPERPOWERS

NOT-TO-DO LIST

_____

_____

_____

_____

_____

_____

_____

_____

_____

_____

_____

_____

_____

_____

_____

_____

_____

_____

_____

_____

_____

_____

_____

BUILDING A TEAM

"The best way to find out if you can trust somebody is to trust them."
–Ernest Hemmingway

"Trust, but verify." **–Ronald Reagan**

Nothing is more frustrating than to have a dream, vision, or plan that no one seems to care about like you do. It is painfully isolating. In a world full of inconsiderate nincompoops, we as entrepreneurs must become experts at bringing quality people into our business or we will never climb above our own limitations.

All through this book you've been really focused on Y-O-U. We determined your baseline, identified your root motivations and started the process of honing your strengths. Now we'll pivot to seeing how your values, motivations and strengths can fit into a bigger picture. Your business.

If I were to sum up the idea of business in one word, I would choose the word relationship. We relate to our clients and customers. We relate to our employees. We relate with our suppliers. Heck, we even relate with the UPS guy that drops off our packages. The problem is that relationship can be challenging or painful.

It's safe to say that we've all had our heart broken and our trust destroyed. Some of us so badly that words like delegation, outsourcing, partnership and networking put a sour taste in our mouth. I'll bet you didn't have to look very far to find that employee who let you down, or the partner that used you for all you were worth. What can I say? People suck, and we need them. How do we find people that don't suck, and how to we manage the fallout when even the non-sucky people let us down?

In the last chapter, we discussed your strengths, SUPERPOWERS, and unique abilities. I harped on you over and over again on your need to focus on your strengths and we established a Not-To-Do List; a lovely list of gaps in your skill set that you need to farm-out to real people that could fail, betray you, and crush your dreams in their evil little hands!

In this chapter we will focus on the importance of building a healthy, supportive team that will bring your incredibly motivated vision to fruition. We will also talk about the practical aspect of building a sound vetting process, so you don't get screwed over any more than you absolutely must. Sound good?

Suicide Squad

If you haven't read or seen The Lord of the Rings, by Tolkien, I highly recommend it. At the center of the story is a golden ring of power, which can give the ability to conquer the world to its wearer. Clearly the ring must be destroyed to prevent evil forces from finding and using it to destroy middle-earth. A meeting is called of all the good kings, battle lords, elves, and dwarfs to recruit the best and the bravest among them, but alas—the mission to destroy the ring is suicide—and no one wants to join the squad. Instead of focusing on the task at hand everyone brings up old offenses, and resentments—basically, it's your average budget meeting.

Amidst the arguing the hobbit with no qualifications volunteers to solve the problem. The wizards and kings knew that Frodo couldn't do it alone, so they volunteered forming the fellowship of the ring setting out to help Frodo fulfill his destiny.

Throughout the story each member of the fellowship gives their gifts, strengths and talents to the cause. In the same way, your business will need an assortment of people on its journey; people with the powers and abilities you lack.

The Honey-Do List

Business owners often think we're the best or the only ones that can do a task right. Maybe we're perfectionist, or maybe entrusting our Why-Baby to someone less invested in the dream has led to poor quality. We'll get to finding better partners, employees in a minute but first I want you to crunch some numbers and begin to understand how you are hurting yourself by not delegating.

A project that is completed 100% of the time at 80% quality is still better than a project completed 20% of the time at 100% quality.

A project that is completed 100% of the time at 80% quality is still better than a project completed 20% of the time at 100% quality.

I know that you are the expert. I know that nobody produces, sells, or handles customers like you but is doing everything really working for you?

What is your success rate with your to-do list? I know that when you do anything on that list, it's going to be done right. How often are you so swamped that you can't get to everything on the list? Is it possible that tasks are missed, or postponed because there are only so many hours in the day? Or, do you get it all done at the cost of your family relationships or your health?

When you're spread too thin it is only a matter of time before the quality of your work suffers. In business it's better done, then perfect.

"Well done is better than well said."—**Benjamin Franklin**

Think again of Sarah, the Pie Lady. What if she had found a way to hire out her accounting to a qualified CPA? She'd be saving herself an hour every day putting in receipts and teaching herself QuickBooks, not to mention the stress of tax time. That same CPA could save her thousands of dollars by avoiding unnecessary taxes, advising her to set up her business as S or C Corporation or an LLC instead of Sole Proprietorship if it's right for her situation and would keep her from accruing unnecessary banking or late fees.

Or she could bring on a college student to bake the pies from 3am to 7am? Imagine how much more enjoyable and productive her life and business could be with a few more hours sleep every night?

Let's talk money too. What if she hired on a marketing professional for straight commission that brought in ten new, loyal customers a week? In six months, that's 260 new customers.

Or, she can hunker down and try to figure it all out on her own by the skin of her teeth and sheer determination.

Tell Me About Yourself

Clearly bringing on help is the path to victory so let's talk about vetting. How can you bring people into your business or venture without sabotaging your dream?

Two words—Personality Tests.

You can ask for references, do background and credit checks but I still believe that the most valuable step to consider when working with anyone is a personality test. I use the same two tests that I offered to you when we were discussing your super powers.

- Myers-Briggs Personality Test
https://www.16personalities.com/personality-types
- DISC Test *https://www.tonyrobbins.com/disc*

Since taking my own tests I've requested that any new hires or partners take the tests too. It gives us all a more comprehensive understanding of each other's preferences, styles and motives. I even find it's helped me to appreciate differences in people that used to really bug me.

Just trust me and make the people take the tests. Just remember to print off your results so you don't lose them.

If the Shoe Fits

Some jobs are better for extroverts, others for introverts. Either of the two tests I mentioned above will give you a clear picture of the types of work any potential hire would excel at, and even more important, what they would totally bomb at.

My team is literally spread across the world, and so is my clientele. It would be very hard for me to get to know them all well enough to understand exactly how their skills, talents and personality could best serve in my goals. The Myers-Briggs Personality Test and the DISC Test have saved me time and heartache by eliminating less than ideal partnerships before they begin.

By taking the time to vet which personalities you hire you'll be better able to fill specific needs. The other option is to go virtual and get cost effective assistance on the internet. Go to *www.fiverr.com, www.guru.com* or *www.freelancer.com* and spend $5, $10, or $20 to have small tasks done for you. It saves me hours of time researching or trying to design graphics.

All My Ex's Live in Texas

Grab a scratch pad and pen. You're going to make a list of the people you've worked with. It doesn't have to exhaustive. Stick to the people that were influential or that you worked closely with or worked together for a long time. Five to ten is plenty.

By influential I mean both good and bad. People that made your life easier and people that made you wish homicide wasn't illegal. Write out anyone you partnered with including volunteer and charity events. I can think of half a dozen people right now, some I'd never want to work with again and some I would gladly work with at the drop of a hat.

Make a column beside each person's name and write down what you loved about working with them. Then make another column and add what you didn't love.

Think of the people you would never want to work with again. What do these people have in common? What are their differences? Why you didn't work well together? This exercise isn't to dredge up the past or make you feel like a jerk. If you were a jerk admit it, take responsibility for your part and forgive yourself. Pay attention what triggered you to play the jerk and avoid people and situations that trigger that in you. It's okay to surround yourself with people that are good for you.

Now look at the people you worked well with. We'll call them the ones that got away. Pay close attention to their similarities and differences. Jot down any patterns you see as a template for any future hires. Were they quiet, loud, funny, or calm in stressful situations? Write it down.

Stay in touch with these people. If you haven't called in a while, drop them a line. Tell them about your business. Give to their ventures with no strings attached. You could be a guest on their Podcast or help them promote what they do by advertising their product in junction with yours. You stand to gain so much more than you give in relationship and support. Don't be an island unto yourself, instead do your life and business with people.

Grass Roots Start Up

Unfortunately, money does not grow on trees. I know, it's a bummer. So, how can you move forward with delegating out your weaknesses when you're broke as a joke?

Let's say you have an awesome product to sell, but you've been beating your head against a wall trying to figure out Facebook ads. Ask around and find someone who is well known for promoting products like yours with ads that convert to actual sales. Then start making calls.

Here's what you say,

"Hey, I have an innovative product that is changing lives around the world! I invested everything I had into production and don't have the capital to pay you for your skills upfront— But I have an interesting solution. What if you market my product for 30 days, and I give you a percentage of my sales? Or... you could market my product for an indefinite amount of time, and I will pay you a large lump sum when we hit these goals.

What do you think?"

If they're an opportunist and can see your business scaling to six or seven figures, in a year or two they may give it a shot.

If they turn you down ask them if they know anyone that would be a good fit for you, or what kind of deal structure would have worked better for them. It's a big world out there and this is a numbers game. Keep asking around until you find someone to help you.

If you think you can't afford a top-notch salesman try offering straight commission with incentives. Tweak the script above to and make sure they understand that the more successful they are closing each sale the sweeter their reward will be. If they're good at their craft and confident in their abilities, they know a success will profit both sides.

If you need a tradesman to make the product the same rules will apply. Make sure your marketing and sales are ready to rock and roll and then paint the picture to your guy that their participation is a no-brainer.

Fr-enemies

What if you could make a strategic alliance with a competitor?

I want you to just think about that for a second. Instead of comparing and worrying about what your competitor is better at or more connected to, you can be focused on what sets you apart. What can you do that other's in your field can't? I'll bet that what you do well would complement what your competitors are doing. Your competitors aren't you and they could benefit from your specific gifts, and talents in their business just as their gifts and talents could greatly benefit yours.

I'm saying you can build a profitable relationship with your competition where you promote them to your audience and vice versa. This kind of partnership can create a lot of anticipation and fresh energy for both businesses. All you need to do is look for frenemies in your industry whose products and services could compliment your own and then partner with them.

I hope that by now I've beaten the idea of the lone wolf, self-made entrepreneur into the ground. Bringing the right people into your business will profit you and your business, given you some tools to help with the vetting and shown you how to hire-in real professionals with no money down or partner with your competition to bring new life and vigor into your business. Be creative and stay open to new possibilities. There are limitless ways to build your network and team.

What I'm going to share with you now is even more powerful than everything I've shared about team building so far. It is a method that will win the heart of any person, anywhere as long as you carry it out it with the right motive.

You Don't Bring Me Flowers Anymore

A few years back I was the random ginger-haired, white guy walking up to a large corporate building, in South Dakota right in the heart of Sioux country. The irritated glare of the receptionist was hot enough to cut glass. I knew what she was thinking, and I was used it. In her mind I was another white man coming to take even more from her people just like many others had done before.

- I was a stranger.
- I didn't call ahead.
- I didn't have an appointment.

But I said one thing, and that secretary immediately stopped what she was doing and walked me past all the other offices until I was standing right in front of the most powerful person in that sovereign nation, the tribal chairman.

Then in one short conversation I would win the business of the entire tribe and solidify a partnership that would last for years to come.

How did I do it?

GIVING

The method I want to share with you earned my previous insurance agency more business relationships with the Sovereign Nations than any other insurance brokerage in the United States. I still use this same technique today to win partnerships, affiliates, networking connections and introductions. It has never failed to open a door. But like I said before, and it bears repeating, it will only work if your motives are pure.

It is no secret that the indigenous tribes of the United States have suffered many injustices. One way to bring honor and respect to a tribe is to acknowledge their reservation is in fact their land and then understanding that coming onto their land, especially to do business without permission, is a great trespass against their tribal government.

When I walked up to the receptionist I said, "Hi, I've come to honor your Chairman with a gift and ask permission to be on your land."

When I got to the Tribal Chairman I would say, "My company and I would like to work with you, but we also understand that this is your Sovereign Nation. I came here today to honor you and your position of authority with a gift, and to ask permission to be on your land."

The Power of a Gift

Why do people hate telemarketers, used car salesmen, and bad MLM's? Because they aren't really trying to help us. No, they are just cheap attempts to get into our wallets. It's like the jerk that expects his date to put out because he bought her dinner. It's gross. It's sleazy. It makes me want to take a shower just thinking about it.

We instantly set ourselves apart from the competition and open the doors to authentic relationship when we give first.

Many times, our first interaction with a tribe was through charitable outreach. We put our money where our mouth was and sponsor community events before we ever made a cent selling them insurance. We made sure that our motive was to gain a lasting, mutually beneficial relationship and for the same reason we didn't swindle our clients. Instead we worked to respect their boundaries, and readily jumped through their red tape as best we could.

If you need a door to open with an affiliate, vendor, influencer or customer base find ways to meaningfully give to them and expect nothing in return. A great book on this subject is *The Dream 100*, by Dana Derricks. It gives a practical approach to reaching and connecting with your target audience through influencers in your industry.

In your business and life, you're going to need to win good people to your cause and sometimes that takes time.

When I was dating my wife, I would bring her a flower every day. On the days I couldn't see her I'd leave a flower on her door step or bedside table if her roommate was home to let me in. I did it every single day and I never missed—even if it meant driving to her house at 11:30pm to drop one off. It may seem a bit extreme, but I did it because I knew she was hurting. She was putting her life together from a major letdown and she was unsure if she was ready to marry me. It was touch and go, but I still brought her a flower every day. I didn't do it to get something from her. I did it so she would know that I was thinking of her and I would wait as long as I had to. The little extra effort I put in to pick and deliver a flower every day has paid off dividends every year since.

The point is that people need to know that we care about them as people. Show your employees and partners that they matter to you. That you're willing to invest in them. Be that guy or gal! Give with no strings attached and watch as your network and community multiply to meet and exceed your every need.

Biological

The Funnel

Social

Four

Psychological

Spiritual

Super
Powers

Not-To-
Do List

UNS
ENTRE
4 ste

Hone
Strengths

The Funnel Four

Determine a
Baseline

ppable
RENEUR

process

Value
Alignment

Life Circle

Identify Root
Motives

7 Levels

ENVIRONMENT

BIOLOGICAL | PSYCHOLOGICAL | SOCIAL | SPIRITUAL

"People overestimate what they can achieve in a year and they underestimate what they can achieve in a decade." – **Tony Robbins**

"I've come to believe that each of us has a personal calling that's as unique as a fingerprint—and that the best way to succeed is to discover what you love and then find a way to offer it to others in the form of service, working hard, and also allowing the energy of the universe to lead you." – **Oprah Winfrey**

We're going to make a major shift in our fourth and final step of the Unstoppable Process. We're pivoting from talking about you to what's around you. Your environment. You need a high-quality environment if you want a high-quality life.

We do this through The Funnel Four. which is our secret sauce. It is how we take your values, motivations and strengths and **recreate your environment** to guarantee lasting fulfillment and success in any area of your life.

For all the implementers out there, get excited. This is where the rubber meets the road and you will start bringing these revelations, strategies and concepts into your world. First, let's talk a little about environment, and how it plays into the last step in becoming Unstoppable.

"When a flower doesn't bloom you fix the environment in which it grows, not the flower." – **Alexander Den Heijer**

Let's say I plant a lemon seed in my yard because I want a lemon tree. I water and fertilize it perfectly but it never sprouts or grows.

Did I do something wrong?

Was my seed defective?

No, there isn't anything wrong with me or the seed. I live in a climate too cold for lemon trees. In fact, as I write this there is fresh snow on the ground and another blizzard in the forecast.

I could be the world's best arborist with a superior lemon seed and my environment would kill the seed.

In the same way, you could take all the work you've done so far in *The Unstoppable Entrepreneur* and start implementing but if your environments aren't healthy and supportive your efforts could be in vain.

Here's a great example: I am an extrovert. I gain energy from time spent with people and lose energy if I'm alone too much. In my insurance business I traveled about half the year and I often stayed in the casinos we served across the country. When I was alone, I wouldn't work as hard or keep up with a healthy diet or workout routine. In a word, I would settle.

My willpower would wane, and, on several occasions, I would find my way down to the poker table. I'd order drinks and make conversation. Maybe for you this doesn't sound like a negative, but for me it was. I would end up staying longer than I had planned, spending more than I intended, drinking more than I wanted and as the night went on, I would become a darker version of myself.

When I worked with a partner, I got more done, my diet and work-outs became a priority and I stayed focused on my goals and values.

At the time I didn't realize how much of my behavior was dictated by my environment. I always thought I had to have stronger willpower to overcome any challenges or issues in my life. When my environment would win over my willpower, I assumed I was just lazy. Now I know that my behavior, while still my choice, was largely influenced by my surroundings.

Years later, you hold a book in your hands begging you to unmask these hidden truths. There are silent killers in your life that are triggered by the environment you are choosing to be in. Improving your environment is the quickest way to inject fresh hope, energy and new ideas into your company. It is how you become an *Unstoppable Entrepreneur*. Neglecting your environment is the fastest way to settle for second best or none at all. In other words, it's the fastest route to failure.

Let me ask you a hypothetical question:

If you were to ride a space shuttle out to the moon and step outside what would happen?

Well, without protection from the environment you would die, right?

Now, let's say you were tough, like the toughest guy on earth and your willpower is the stuff of legends.

Would any of that make a difference?

No, it wouldn't. The moon's environment doesn't have what you need to live. It doesn't matter how strong you are, your daily environment is either adding to your health, success and emotional well-being or draining it.

It doesn't matter how strong you are, your daily environment is either adding to your health, success and emotional well-being or draining it.

If your world isn't giving you what you need to succeed eventually the willpower will run out and you will stop. That's why being *The Unstoppable Entrepreneur's* isn't about willpower, it's about knowing who you are, what moves you and what you excel at and then using all that information to craft an environment that sustains forward motion.

...being The Unstoppable Entrepreneur isn't about willpower, it's about knowing who you are, what moves you and what you excel at and then using all that information to craft an environment that sustains forward motion.

It is a well perpetuated myth that we succeed by overcoming our environment.

No, no, NO!

The truth is that we are all a product of our environment.

If you haven't put much thought into your environment, chances are it's working against your greater good. A well-crafted environment makes greatness, and a thoughtless environment produces mediocrity.

If you're ready to live a life based on your values, motivations, utilizing your strengths then it begins by intentionally taking back your environments through the Funnel Four.

Love is a Battlefield

Bombs are exploding all around you. You're knee deep in mud and smoke, in a field of ditches and barbed wire. Your comrades are falling all around you. You're wounded, hungry, exhausted and almost out of ammunition.

This is the battle for your fulfillment—and it's happening all around you.

Up until this point everything we've done has been to put bullets in your gun. Your values, motivations and strengths are your ammunition. They will shred your opposition and carve out your way to the win; but there is more to war than blowing things up and shooting off rounds.

Location, location, location...

A soldier on the battlefield is always paying attention to potential traps, ambushes and cover. They don't just run into battle shooting. Instead, they take in their surroundings and choose where they will engage. In the same way you need to become strategic about your surroundings. You need to think like a general and put yourself in the best possible situation for victory.

From now on, your environments are either low ground or high ground.

They're either helping you to win the battle of fulfillment or lose it. The Funnel Four is how we take your four environments and systematically stack the deck in your favor. It's how you will stay on higher ground and set yourself up for optimal success.

The Four Environments

Before we bust into the Funnel Four let's clarify what the four environments are;

Biology, Psychology, Social, & Spiritual.

These four arenas are where the choices are made, steps are taken, and victories won. They are where the battle takes place and they each will act as a source of energy or a drain.

Let's begin.

Biology

ALL THINGS PERTAINING TO YOUR PHYSICAL SURROUNDINGS AND THE HEALTH OF YOUR MIND AND BODY.

Biological issues are the first thing I listen for when I'm consulting with a client for the first time. Why? Because it is the simplest explanation and solution. If you have an imbalance or struggle because of hormones, disease, injury or malnutrition, then your improvement is relatively straight forward. If you are expressing feelings of being overwhelmed or anxious, I'd ask about your living situation, relationships, diet and sleep patterns. I'd also start digging for clues of a mental health issue.

Have you ever forgotten to fill up your gas tank and run out on the side of the road? I have, and honestly, I felt like such an idiot. I had gotten busy and distracted and out in the middle of nowhere, my car putted to a stop on the side of the highway. It was a huge inconvenience, but do you think I got mad at my car for not running without fuel? Of course not. Cars can't run without fuel—they can't even run if their fuel is contaminated.

I had a friend with a brand-new diesel car. He loaned it to his younger sister-in-law, and she called him a few hours later saying his car had died on the interstate… Why? She had mistakenly filled the tank with gasoline, which costed him a tow back to the mechanics and a couple thousand bucks for a new fuel system. We have to be careful what we put in the tank, right?

Why don't we get this when it comes to our own bodies? We know that processed carbs and sugar aren't good for us. We know that junk food is… well, junk. How is it that we fill ourselves up with low quality food and then expect to run on all cylinders?

You eat three donuts from the break room every morning and by lunch you're tired, starving and have a migraine. Then you have the gall to say that you think it's genetic! Are you kidding me? Alright, fine—maybe there is a genetic disposition in your family but you're also putting the wrong fuel into your body!

Taking care of your body is paramount to achieving your business goals. Your physical body is literally the only way to bring your ideas into the world, either through words or actions. To quote my wife's favorite movie of all time,

"If you don't have your health, you don't have anything." – **The Princess Bride.**

Most of the entrepreneurs I work with put their business and/or family before their own health. Many are practicing bad habits like:
- eating junk food,
- not getting enough sleep,
- not drinking enough water,
- allowing constant stress with no limits.

Habits like these are not just bad for your energy level or your waistline; first and foremost, it absolutely cripples your mind. As an innovative and creative entrepreneur, remember that your brain is truly the core of your business. It isn't only at the core, or part of the core— your brain is "the central nervous system" that your business depends on. If your brain fails, everything fails.

Listen to Rich's story below and I promise you'll never look at your brain the same way again.

Rich is a friend of mine that owns a handyman business North of Seattle. A few years back in the prime of his life and in the peak of the construction and remodel season he began to experience fierce, migraine headaches. In no time at all they morphed into extreme vertigo, dizzy spells and what looked like the early stages of dementia. The brain fog was heavy. It was like he aged forty years over a weekend. Before long he could hardly get out of bed. He was losing clients because he couldn't work and whenever I saw him, he looked worse. He went to the doctor, did tests, and saw specialists, but they couldn't find the cause. They said he looked fine on paper, but he continued to deteriorate until he could hardly leave his house. Terrified that they would soon lose Rich to an unexplained disease his wife and three children braced for the worst. On top of it all they lost their home and had to relocate to a smaller apartment across town. Two days after the move, his symptoms completely resolved. He was perfectly healthy again. It turned out that the house they had been living in was riddled with mold that was hidden in the walls. Rich's symptoms were caused by mold toxicity in his central nervous system.

Your physical environment has a direct impact on your health especially the health of your brain. Rich's symptoms were caused by a toxic environment that affected his brain making his healthy, strong body unusable.

While I do talk a little on diet and other health related topics, I deliberately focus on brain health because there is a cavernous lack of real information on brain health and function in the entrepreneurial community.

"Change your brain, change your life." – **Daniel Amen**

Your brain is a hunk of fatty tissue that is responsible for the consumption of 40% of the calories you take in. If you're eating junk, then your brain is running on junk. You get junk thoughts, junk concentration and junk decisions. It is a downward spiral and the first step out of the vortex is prioritizing your brain health.

On the Spectrum

Nobody's brain is picture-perfect so instead of good or bad let's think of brain health on a spectrum from healthy to unhealthy. As entrepreneurs we need our brains functioning at the highest level possible. Think about it... The human heart pumps blood most efficiently when it's healthy. Our livers and kidneys fulfill their cleansing duties when they are healthy. How can we expect our brains to function at peak levels without supporting their health needs?

If something that seems as trivial as air quality affects your performance then what about your diet, morning routine, relationships, and use of technology? Where you are, what you take in—it all affects your brain.

Start With Food

How do we take the higher ground in our biological environment? We start with what we can actively control.

That's right, you start with what you eat. Why, because it's what you have complete, direct control over. Unless you're a spoon-fed toddler, you choose what goes in your mouth. It's time to make those choices work in your favor.

Diet plans and advice are as abundant as the stars. My wife and I both benefit from eating a low carb, high fat/protein diet based in plenty of fresh fruits and vegetables. We don't eat gluten, dairy or refined sugars because of allergy and inflammation issues in our family. Your ideal diet may be very different from ours, but we recommend removing processed foods and sugar and increasing nutrient rich foods like leafy greens and fish.

Once you're eating like a champion and treating food like fuel then you can start to identify what other environmental factors could be draining your health. There is a long list of recommended blood tests that you can request from your primary care physician to help you identify deficits in your vitamin, mineral, hormones, etc... Involve your doctor as you investigate for possible sources of inflammation in your home environment like allergens, pet dander, pollen, or mold. Inflammation is not your friend and the more you do to eliminate it the better you will feel and perform.

Healing a Broken Mind

"We're all broken. That's how the light gets in." – **Author Unknown**

What if your brain has sustained damage? Maybe you've used drugs, hit your head a lot in the boxing ring or got in a serious car accident. The outcome of those types of things can be visually seen in your brain today.

My wife got into Daniel Amen after reading his book, *Unleashing the Power of the Female Brain*, and years later when my insomnia and migraines worsened, she pressed hard for me to invest in my brain health. I couldn't sleep and was waking up an average of 15 times a night. The horrible, debilitating migraines I endured a couple times a week were so intense I worried that I had a brain tumor. So, I did my questionnaires, underwent a thorough examination and in 2015 I had a SPECT Brain Scan done at the Amen Clinic.

It was crazy seeing inside my own head. The doctors showed me the physical markers in my brain. I saw the damage done by concussions I suffered in football and soccer. They showed me the tell-tale markers for ADHD that explained my difficulty concentrating and the increased blood flow in my pre-frontal cortex that indicated anxiety and depression. They told me I had the brain of a CEO and despite all my shortcomings my brain was above average, but that wasn't what rocked my world.

You see I began using drugs and alcohol in middle school. I'd cut back and quit several times as an adult but never experienced lasting sobriety. Seeing my brain was an incredible life-changing experience for me. In the flip of a page I saw what drugs and alcohol had really done for me.

My choice to use drugs and abuse alcohol had injured portions of my brain making a small portion in the top, center look like decomposing swiss cheese.

I could never adequately express the regret I felt in that moment. But, I am grateful for the experience that made me take a long hard look at my life and my choices. A look that I hope you take as well. If you struggle with substance abuse or compulsive behaviors, I strongly recommend that you begin your recovery in your brain. The fight for sobriety begins with a healthy mind.

If you're in anyway curious or concerned about your brain health, I'd recommend checking out Dr. Daniel Amen. On his site at *www.brainhealthassessment.com* you can take a free quiz that will give you a stronger understanding of your brain's strengths and weaknesses.

Stack the Deck

Once you've done what you can with your physical health take a look at your surroundings and make sure your environment makes the changes you seek inevitable.

Rachel used to be a HUGE sugar fiend. The term addict really doesn't do it justice. She baked sweets all the time, making caramel and truffles from scratch. There was always something to expand my waistline on the kitchen counter. Baking was a stress relief for her. All that changed when, a while back, she read a book by Benjamin Hardy called *Willpower Doesn't Work*. Chapter six in this book was about removing everything from your environment that conflicts with your goals and values. Basically, the book said to go into your kitchen with a garbage bag and throw out or donate everything you shouldn't be eating. That really stuck with her and a few months later she did it.

Today there are no processed sugars in our house, just natural alternatives like dates, agave, honey and pure maple syrup. She lost twenty pounds in a couple months but more importantly she was able to resolve chronic joint pain caused by inflammation.

She had tried to quit sugar many times before and had always failed because she didn't craft her environment—the deck was stacked against her. In the battle for her health she needed to take the higher ground. She had to make winning automatic. That meant removing the option of losing. You must do the same in your health and home.

If your goal is to eliminate sugar from your diet and a canister of sugar sits on the kitchen counter, the deck is not stacked in your favor and your environment will win.

Stack your physical environment to suit your goals and values. Don't allow things that conflict with your values into your home and you will make winning automatic.

PSYCHOLOGY

ALL THINGS PERTAINING TO YOUR IDENTITY, SENSE OF WORTH AND PERSONAL POWER.

What you think about yourself is the primary concern of the psychological environment. Internally you'll deal with your thought life. Externally you'll consider how your physical environment is helping or hurting your self-image. Thoughts are powerful and habit forming.

There was a farmer who drove out to feed his cattle twice a day for forty years. It got to be that he didn't need to steer his tractor because the twice daily trip had worn deep ruts into the path. He eventually could just put it into gear and it would steer itself to and from the feeding spot for the livestock. One rainy spring it got so bad that the farmer couldn't get his tractor out of the ruts to any other part of the farm.

Our thought patterns are just like those ruts. If we think a negative thought once it's like driving the tractor over muddy ground, and the more we think negative thoughts, the deeper the ruts in our mind go. Each despairing thought makes it more and more difficult to choose healthy, balanced, and/or hopeful thoughts. The same can be said for healthy, positive thought patterns.

If you have the habit of talking down to yourself consider pulling that tractor out of the mud and starting some empowering new ruts. It's a lot of work in the beginning but once you've established the habit, it will almost run on autopilot.

In this section we're going to get specific about what psychological environments bring greatness out of you.

Force Yourself to Greatness

If you played football in high school, you'll remember the two-a-day practices in August. They were hot, sweaty and grueling. Remember the camaraderie? The goading of your teammates, the growls of your coaches to do it right this time! Shouting in your face in the huddle—you went from being a pubescent boy to a warrior! At least in your mind.

Now, imagine if you had been asked to do those same drills, workouts, and practice routes on your own, at home in your backyard. Do you think you would have been even half as effective when game time came along? Heck no! Your coaches created a psychological environment that shifted your mindset. You were no longer one single player. You were one of the team.

How can you craft the same type of psychological environment to propel yourself and your business to success?

Be Your Biggest Fan

A true fan would never allow anyone to disrespect their team. It's time that you became that kind of fan—for yourself.

Attack anything that damages your self-image. Nothing is more important than what you think of you. Build yourself up with affirmations and take negative thoughts captive. Remember, this is a war. Allowing negative thoughts to roam in your head would be like allowing an enemy assassin into your strategic headquarters.

It's time to take back your thought life and become your biggest supporter. Post the affirmations from your 7 Levels and read it meaningfully to yourself every morning before you start your day. After a while, just like the farmer driving in his ruts, it will become second nature. Another book I've found extremely helpful in this arena is *The Miracle Morning*, by Hal Elrod. His approach to the morning routine has transformed millions around the globe.

Where You Work Matters

Often entrepreneurs will put their desks against a dark wall in their basement and wonder why they don't feel inspired. Your brain is responding to the cues you're giving it. Dark means sleep and facing a wall with no windows can make you feel trapped.

What's Around You Matters

Look around your office. Is there anything here that makes you feel "less than" or like a failure. I don't care if it's a picture of your mother, your unframed diploma, a book you never read, a clay sculpture from your kids, or a stack of bills—relocate them. Your workplace is now a shrine to your unique greatness, and ability. Everything on the walls should fortify and inspire you. Everything you see and touch should remind you of your own power and potential. You should feel like a million bucks every time you walk in.

If you're unsure about your workspace, or not big on aesthetics I have a quick little exercise you can try.

I want you to imagine yourself in ten years having succeeded in every goal you've placed for yourself. How do you look, what are you wearing? Now, imagine that successful and fulfilled future-self walking into your current workspace. Is it worthy of them? Does it show them the respect they deserve? If it doesn't then change it. Give yourself the respect you deserve, and you'll accomplish more.

THE UNSTOPPABLE ENTREPRENEUR

Owning a business is tough. Don't make it tougher by piling on mental blocks. Remove the negative cues and replace them with positive ones.

Where's the Fight?

Like I said in the last section, there is a cavernous lack of understanding on brain health in the entrepreneurial field.

You would never know by looking at her, but my wife has hidden a lifetime of depression and suicidal thoughts behind a smile. When we were first dating, she told me that even in her earliest childhood memories she would wake up on a beautiful, sunny morning and her first thought would be to kill herself. She was only 8-years-old when she tried to hang herself with her jump rope. She self-harmed in high school and had other suicide attempts as a teenager and young adult. Her symptoms were chronic and severe.

As she grew up, she got bad advice from unqualified, well-meaning people. Advice that may have been appropriate for someone not struggling with clinical depression. She was told to work on controlling her thoughts, and only think on good things. To memorize and quote scriptures having to do with depression. To pray more and to take the attention off herself by giving to the less fortunate. These were great suggestions for a mild case of the blues, but it almost cost Rachel her life.

Rather than seeking medical treatment for her depression my wife redoubled her efforts to out-think her depression. She worked tirelessly every day, with limited success, to not be suicidal. She found ways to deal with her mind but when she hit 30 her symptoms spiraled out of control. Everything she'd done—diet, exercise, counseling, prayer, meditation—the life she'd built to keep her mind in check wasn't enough. She began to have sudden, severe suicidal thoughts and the urge to hit our kids, and that's when she called the doctor.

Her doctor was amazed she'd lived with such severe symptoms so long without help. This battle wasn't psychological, it was biological. The reality is that my wife couldn't have talked herself out of her depression any more than you can talk yourself out of a broken arm or a vitamin D deficiency. She needed a biological solution.

If you struggle with anxiety, depression or other mental health issues consider that you could be fighting your battle on the wrong front. You could do everything I've recommended and have little to no success.

If that's true, your mental health issues may be biological instead of psychological. Your victory may be waiting on another battleground.

As you read her story do you see glimpses of yourself or someone you love? I would encourage you to seek professional counsel and make sure you're fighting on the right battlefield.

SOCIAL

HOW YOU INTERACT AND RELATE TO THOSE AROUND YOU.

A Lion Runs with Other Lions

"Don't run with the easy crowd, get yourself around and surrounded by people who will force you to grow."
– Jim Rohn

I've heard it said that if four of your closest friends have filed bankruptcy, you'll be the fifth. The people you surround yourself with will influence your life's direction. To put it simply, show me your friends and I'll show you your future.

…show me your friends and I'll show you your future.

If all your friends are divorced and their kids hate them it won't be long before you're right there with them. The opposite can be true as well. If your friends value their families and relationships, it's bound to rub off on you. It goes deeper than social interaction. Your associations affect every area of your well-being.

Are you unhappy with your health or diet? Look at the diet and health of the five people you spend the most time with. If they are sicker than you then it's time to march over to a gym and make some new friends.

Are you always broke? Stop hanging out with broke people and start spending more time with people who know how to increase wealth.

Do you feel stuck in life? Then take a class, join a community group or committee. You're bound to find people who are going after their dreams and passions. Make them a priority in your life.

Remember that you are in a battle for fulfillment. It is essential to get yourself in a healthy social environment. People whose lives align with your values, are on your side. Those whose lives don't align with your values, are not.

Now that doesn't mean you go ballistic and cut off family or other relationships for good just because you have different values or goals. No, it means that those people shouldn't be in your top five.

The High Five

You will grow as fast as your social environment will allow for. Like a good connoisseur, you need to carefully curate the five people you choose to spend time with outside of your immediate family—spouse and kids.

Purposely choose to spend time with people that would push you towards growth, not those who would pull you away from growth.

The most successful business people find a way to get access to mastermind groups, conferences, and other opportunities. They make time to associate with the big thinkers and world changers of their industries.

So, what do you look for as you choose your High Five?

"Great minds discuss ideas;
Average minds discuss events;
Small minds discuss people." – -**Unknown**

Surround yourself with people who have ideas. Don't waste time with people that are more negative than positive or indulge in a bunch of gossip. Love them from a distance and make your social environment as healthy as possible by choosing people who value you and support your dreams.

SPIRITUAL

YOUR SENSE OF
MEANING AND PURPOSE.
CONNECTION TO GOD,
PAST (HERITAGE),
PRESENT (MINDFULNESS),
FUTURE (LEGACY)

The battle for fulfillment begins in our pocketbook.... Just kidding. If that were true the wealthiest people in the world would be the happiest, most fulfilled people in the world. While some of them are very happy, fulfilled people, far too many business owners arrive at "success" and find it an empty shell. How is that possible? It's possible because the battle for fulfillment and meaning begins in the intangible spiritual.

Don't lose me here, I promise not to get all weird and spooky on you. We as entrepreneurs, live in an age of opportunity. It is a virtual theme park of technology that has made it possible to affect change across the globe on a scale never before seen in history. The world is literally our playground, but without a real reason to be here we could miss the joy. Having a purpose that is in fact bigger than you is your life line in the midnight of your struggle. You were certainly born for something unique and purposeful.

Your spiritual environment is where the struggle for authenticity is won. As we take a minute to discuss spirituality, I want you to realize that it envelops more than visiting your preferred place of worship.

Spirituality isn't just world view or religion. It's also about your connection to your heritage and future legacy.

Spirituality is all about discovering your sense of meaning and purpose—your place in this life. It's where you discover who you are.

Spirituality is where you get to answer questions like, "Why does my life matter?" or "What is my purpose?" These connections are what bring meaning to your life.

If religion makes you uncomfortable than think of the spiritual environment as a place of connectedness and reflection.

Who are you in relationship to God?
The World?
Your ancestors?
Your heritage?
Your current and future family?

Spirituality is the most commonly over looked solution. My relationship with my Creator has revolutionized not just my life but my business.

In the beginning my business was deeply tied to my sense of worth. If we were doing well, closing deals and gaining accolades I would feel worthy. My sense of worth was tied to my performance, and failure crippled me. In a way, my business became my God. A harsh master that lorded over me. I reached a tipping point where my need for peace and meaning overcame my fear of failure and I stepped back from my business for a reality check.

Our creator never intended us to live in slavery to our finances, aspirations or status.

When we climb to the highest peaks of success and find them void of meaning, God stands beside us. He is trying to get our attention.

We are not what we do.

You are not what you do—you are more.

You are a unique, gifted, wonderful human being.

Connecting to your history, your legacy and to God brings you into harmony with your place in this world. God has designed a place for you; a place you do not need to earn.

When I finally realized that I was accepted and appreciated regardless of my contribution I was able to run my business instead of being run by my business.

When we "walk in our purpose", business becomes a means to an end in our life and legacy. A tool for our life's work.

I personally believe God wants to be involved in every area of our life, love on us and bless everything we do. It's a relationship you're greatly missing out on if it's not your priority.

Can you see how important your spiritual life is to your business? We can keep our feet firmly planted in the physical world and at the same time admit that our lives are a profoundly spiritual journey. Understanding that you are not the center of the universe can have a calming effect.

Conclusion

Learning without implementation won't do you any good. As informative and engaging as *The Unstoppable Entrepreneur* is, please believe me when I say that my wife and I didn't write this book for our own amusement! (Few people would find the process of writing a book with their spouse amusing, and we are not the exception).

As I said in the beginning, the heroes of our industries, business or otherwise weren't born successful and determined. No, they started out much like the rest of us. They had to learn and grow and before they became the incredible force they are today. They had to become…

We wrote this book to shave years off your becoming. The four-step process, when combined with honest and determined action will make a real lasting difference in your life. Let our work throughout these pages become your guide. Let the concepts and strategies sink in and produce genuine, heartfelt direction and meaning in your life. Whenever you feel the cold hand of indifference wrapping around your life, take out this book and remember who you are.

Whenever you forget why you dared greatly, take this book out and remember what you want. Whenever you want to revive your passion, take out this book and remember what makes you feel alive.

Every time you read this book it will wake up your sleepy WHY-baby rekindling your unique drive and ambition.

Let me share with you our why, our reason for writing this book. My wife and I value life. Every life is important to us, because we've both been touched by the epidemic of suicide. Our desire is to bring hope, practical solutions and purpose to those who have lost their way. To accomplish this we need you, our incredible reader, to find and walk in your purpose. You see, it is your testimonial of life-change we're after. We want to receive your email or letter, or have you stop us in the airport, or grocery store to tell us about your transformation. How the strategies and ideas expressed in this book gave you hope, practical solutions and purpose. Only then, will we know that we accomplished our goal of changed lives.

For you to get those awesome results (and us our testimonial), you'll have to do the hard work of self-discovery and acceptance. All the tools you need are already in your hands. The power to change your life is yours, and we want you to carpe diem.

Defined by Merriam-Webster: This Latin phrase, which literally means "pluck the day," was used by the Roman poet Horace to express the idea that we should enjoy life while we can.

You know the secret to a fulfilled, purposeful life. You have no excuse. Like us you will refuse to buy into the fluff, and hype of social media influence. You'll see the deeper needs layered beneath artificial grabs at achievement. Instead of being pushed and pulled into every new fashion, you will stay centered on who you are and what you want in this life. You know that fulfillment isn't a place, or a destination but a path we choose to walk every day. It is that same choice to stay true to your values, motivations, gifts and environment that will carry you to heights of determination and fulfillment seldom realized in our consumer driven world. It will be incredible.

We want to share one more thing with you. Whenever we've lacked something in life, we focus our energies on giving to others. If we need more encouragement, we find people who need encouraging and we give them the encouragement we have. If we need hope or success, we find ways to give those things to the people God has put right in front of us. You never have to look far to find someone who could use a smile or a kind word.

The love and kindness we give without strings attached has a funny way of coming back to us; in good time. One of my favorite verses of scripture is found in the NLT of Galatians 6:7

"Don't be misled—you cannot mock the justice of God. You will always harvest what you plant."

The truth is that any gift you give will multiply back to you.

I would encourage you to adopt the same approach to areas of need in your life. If you've found value in this book, if it's helped you in any way, consider giving a copy to five people you care about and want greater fulfillment and success for. It could be relatives, friends, coworkers or acquaintances, or someone you just met and want to have a profound impact on. It may sound like this benefits us, and it does. Sure, we'll sell more books, but you'll also be giving us the opportunity to touch another life.

Every book purchased is the hope of another prevented suicide. It's the possibility of another thriving, fulfilled business owner, or marriage, or parent. It's another person using their retirement years to build a meaningful legacy that will stand for generations to come.

Our goal is to make a difference in millions of peoples lives, but to do that, we need your help. And we give you this promise: You will benefit the most. Choosing to help someone else to find their direction and motivation in life is the beginning of your path to fulfillment. And at the same time, you will be making a marked difference in their life. Your gift will go on to impact their family, friends and circle of influence. This book could forever alter the course of someone's life and it could be you that gives it to them. Without you, they may never find these truths.

Write down five people you will give a copy of this book to:

1. _____

2. _____

3. _____

4. _____

5. _____

It has been the honor of a lifetime to speak into your life! We look forward to hearing your success story.

To your future!

Stephen and Rachel

Get more tools, join the partner community and take the;
Unstoppable 30 Day Challenge at
www.unstoppablejacksons.com

Acknowledgments

To all the risk takers out their who've been a part of my journey. Thank you for sharing your successes and failures. An entrepreneur's journey can be glamorous, but also full of hard work, misunderstandings, turmoil, disappointment and relationship issues within ourselves and with others. Thank you, for being vulnerable with your real-life struggles and victories. It brings hope to our journey.

Thank you to Dana and Akbar for your forwards. Your inspiration to me and Rachel has personally motivated and corrected our journey. You're changing the lives of thousands all over the globe.

Thank you, Rachel, for standing by me in my darkest hour and being my rock. I still can't believe you married me, and I'm so glad you did. I'd also like to thank my ginger ninjas, Nathanael, Isaac and Ben. You are the greatest blessings in my life, and I am proud of each of you. But I can still kick your butts at Super Smash Bros.

Thank you, Valerie Woelk, for the hours of editing, formatting, phone calls and inspiration but most importantly for letting me marry your daughter. You're the best mother-in-law anyone could ask for.

Thank you, to my mother Sandi Shirley, who sacrificed all, for my brothers and I, you're truly the most beautiful flower.

Thank you, to my pastors and mentors, past and present. Especially, ET & LaFaye Tapper, Mike Walsh and Nick Nicolls for mentoring me in the most important thing, my relationship with Christ.

I'd also like to send a special thank you to Shane & Jessica Lewis for introducing us to Celebrate Recovery; John & Cheryl Baker, Mac & Mary Own and the Incredible National Team and all of our forever family across the globe. You've taught me what it means to be a grateful believer.

Stephen

I, heartedly second all of the gratitude in my husband's acknowledgements.

To (Stephen), you are the man for me—everyday, all day, 365. You have been the greatest catalyst of positive change and growth in my life since the moment we met. You believed in me when I didn't. You encouraged me when I couldn't. And you've made me laugh when I wanted to cry. You drive me crazy! You are incredible, and I am so proud of you.

To my boys, you are my constant joy. Thank you, for understanding when I had to work on the book late into the night. Thank you, for helping when I was stressed about deadlines and rewrites. You are precious and perfect. And as promised, now that the book is finally done, YOU'RE GOING to Disneyland.

Mom, I will never pay the debt of gratitude I owe you. You are my best friend, my pillar of strength and my favorite shoulder to cry on. You make the world better by being in it. You showed me how to live, to love and to find beauty in everything. You've given me the gift of appreciation.

Joanna, you're my person. Your goodness has made me believe in friendship again. Thank you, for always being only a phone call away. Now, let's get tattoos!

Most importantly I want to thank Jesus, my Creator, my Lord, my Savior and my Friend. You are my light. You are my hope. You never gave up on me. I live because You live in me. Thank you, for the opportunity to write this book together with Stephen. I pray that it would touch the lost, hopeless and downtrodden and give them the grace and strength to believe in their dreams again. Psalm 126

My last thank you is to you, my reader. You are a gift to me. There were countless nights where I stared distraught and cross eyed at the keyboard trying to co-write this manuscript with my spouse. What got me through was the hope of you. The possibility of your life improving, of your dreams coming to fruition. That is what gave me the courage to finish. You are a beautiful part of the world and I am profoundly grateful to be a part of your journey.

Rachel

CPSIA information can be obtained
at www.ICGtesting.com
Printed in the USA
BVHW041647110319
542318BV00012B/1171/P